Murder in Co

A Play

Philip King
and
John Boland

Samuel French - London
New York - Toronto - Hollywood

ISBN 0 573 01289 X

CHARACTERS

Alan Wilson
Margaret Stephens
Ted Smith
Philip Stephens
Ronnie Meadows
Phoebe Kershaw
Patricia Robins
Doris Stewart

The action of the play passes in a Church Hall
in a small town

ACT I
  A Night in February, 7.15 p.m.

ACT II
  Fifteen minutes later

ACT III
  A fortnight later, 7.45 p.m.

Time – the present

MURDER IN COMPANY

Produced by **Theatre South East** at the DE LA WARR PAVILION, BEXHILL-ON-SEA, on the 21st September 1972, with the following cast of characters:

Alan Wilson	Alan Buckman
Margaret Stephens	Barbara Farrell
Ted Smith	David Masterman
Philip Stephens	Richard Burnett
Ronnie Meadows	Alan Granville
Phoebe Kershaw	Peggy Paige
Patricia Robins	Virginia Moore
Doris Stewart	Janice Hoskins

Directed by Michael ffoulkes

Amateur Premiere by the Southwick Players at the Barn Theatre, Southwick, Sussex, on 13th March 1973, with the following cast:

Alan Wilson	Robin Burch
Margaret Stephens	Sue Geere
Ted Smith	Roy Twine
Philip Stephens	Philip King
Ronnie Meadows	Stanley Jones
Phoebe Kershaw	Peggy Deall
Patricia Robins	Elizabeth Flower
Doris Stewart	Pamela Grey

Directed by Philip King

ACT I

The bare stage of a Church Hall, 7.15 on a night in February

The back wall of the stage is visible, but the sides are masked with draw curtains which act as wings. One or two folded whist tables and a small form are up against the back wall, other forms and bentwood chairs are piled up near them. There are steps leading from the stage to the auditorium

When the CURTAIN *rises, the stage is in almost total darkness—the only light coming from an extremely feeble and very dirty bulb hanging by a flex from the flies. Down stage, with his back to the audience, sitting in a bentwood chair, is a male figure (though in the dim light the audience could be in doubt as to whether it is male or female) wearing a duffle coat with the hood almost covering the head. He sits quite motionless for a while*

After a pause there is a door slam off L. *The figure rises, moves uncertainly for a split second without turning to the audience, then darts off* R *behind one of the draw curtains. After another pause Margaret Stephens enters* L. *She is an attractive woman of thirty to thirty-five, though this is not discernible in the low light. She moves slowly* C, *hesitates, then looks at her wrist-watch, takes a script from her largish handbag, opens it, but after looking at the dismal light above her head, throws the script on a chair, pulls the chair beneath the light and sits down to read the script putting her handbag on the floor*

Alan Wilson, the duffle-coated figure, emerges from behind the curtain stealthily, holding a scarf. He is a pleasant young man of twenty-one. He creeps behind Margaret and throws the scarf round her neck. She gives a really terrified scream

Alan (*through Margaret's scream*) Got you!

Margaret's scream tails off into a moan. Her head almost sags forward

(*Seeing this, alarmed*) Margaret! Margaret! You're—you're all right, aren't you? (*He releases the curtain quickly and puts his arms round Margaret*)
Margaret (*in a just audible voice*) You fool! You damned young fool! (*She is still giving little gasps*)
Alan Darling, I'm sorry. I—I—I didn't mean—(*still holding her*)—I didn't mean to frighten you . . . not really frighten you, I mean. It was just— just a joke.
Margaret (*weakly*) A joke!
Alan But you knew it was *me*, didn't you?

Margaret (*gradually pulling herself together*) I suppose I did, but . . .
Alan We'd arranged to meet here early.
Margaret Yes, but . . . (*Still shaken*) Oh! Give me a minute to pull myself together.
Alan (*after a slight pause*) Margaret, darling . . .
Margaret Alan, this is madness; and it's asking for trouble. If Philip . . .
Alan Damn Philip! He's nothing but a bullying, bombastic swine!
Margaret (*sharply*) He's my husband!
Alan But you don't love him. How can you—the way he treats you? You love me; you know you do. (*He puts his arms around her*)
Margaret (*desperately*) Alan—please—let me go. This has got to stop I tell you!
Alan (*his arms tightening around her; almost in a shout*) No!
Margaret (*weakly*) It's—it's insane. (*She yields to his embrace*)

Suddenly the lights in the auditorium come up. Alan and Margaret break away with little gasps of alarm

Almost as soon as the lights come up, the voice of Ted Smith is heard from the back of the hall

Smith (*fairly loudly*) Hey! Hey! What's all this?

The two on stage do not reply. They stand looking very embarrassed. Smith walks down the auditorium. He is a ferrety-looking, not too clean, individual of around forty years of age, in working clothes. When half-way down the hall, he speaks again

(*Sarcastically*) Bit before your time, aren't you?
Alan (*still shaken, but trying to put a face on*) I beg your pardon?
Smith You 'eard. Night bookin's in this 'all are from seven-thirty till ten-thirty.
Alan Well, what about it?
Smith It isn't seven-thirty yet—only a quarter-past. You're trespassing—that's what about it.
Alan (*angrily*) Don't talk such . . .
Margaret (*under her breath, restraining him*) Alan—don't . . .
Smith (*to Alan*) Such *what*, son? (*With a grin*) I suppose you'd tell me if this wasn't a church 'all—and if there wasn't a lady present. (*Under his breath*) Lady! (*He comes up the steps on to the stage*)
Alan (*making a move towards Smith*) Why you . . . !
Margaret (*again restraining him*) Alan . . . !

Smith, now well on stage, looks towards the others knowingly. He stands quite at ease for a moment or two, enjoying their discomfiture

Smith (*at last, easily*) Well—seein' you *are* 'ere . . .

Smith exits L

Margaret and Alan follow him with their eyes. The Lights come up in battens and floats; the House Lights go out

Smith returns

(*Continuing with a grin*) Don't want to be gropin' about in the dark, d'you? (*Meaningly*) Or—er . . . ? (*He gives a false embarrassed cough. After a slight pause*) Let's see. You're the Dr'matic Society, aren't you?
Margaret Yes.
Smith I've only been caretaker 'ere a week yet, so I'm a bit muddled up with all you people re'earsalin'. Dr'matic Society, Op'ratic Society, Choral Society. (*After a slight pause*) But you're the Dr'matic Society, eh?
Alan (*curtly*) Two of it—not all of it.

Margaret looks at Alan warningly

Smith (*with his eyes on Alan*) Funny, aren't you? Bet you don't 'alf make 'em laugh out there. (*With a nod of his head towards the auditorium. After a slight pause*) Yes, of course! I remember now.
Alan Remember what?
Smith *Your* faces. I've a good memory for faces.

Margaret and Alan look at him, blankly

Last Friday night, after the Vicar 'ad offered me the job, he brought me 'ere to show me my duties—so to speak. You lot were just finishin' re'earsalin'—we stood at the back of the 'all till you'd stopped. That's when I saw you. Int'restin', isn't it? (*He pauses, then turns to Alan with a thin smile*) Wouldn't 'appen to 'ave a cigarette on you by any chance?
Alan (*curtly*) I don't smoke.
Smith H'm! (*With a look towards Margaret*) Bit young for it, eh?
Margaret (*quickly*) I have some. (*She dives into her bag and produces an opened packet·of cork-tipped cigarettes and holds it out to Smith*)
Smith (*coolly*) Ta! I seem to've run out. (*As he takes one*) An' you don't seem to 'ave many either. Pity 'cos I was goin' to ask you if you could . . .
Margaret (*after a quick look at Smith*) I meant to get some more on the way here. (*To him, hesitantly*) Alan—would you mind?
Alan What?
Margaret I expect the shop at the corner of the street's still open. Would you mind poppin'g along there and getting me twenty——
Smith (*cutting in, easily*) Not keen on these cork-tipped things myself.
Margaret (*again looking towards Smith, then to Alan*) —twenty Embassy Plain.
Alan But, look here . . . !
Margaret (*almost pleadingly*) Alan, please. (*Diving into her bag, again*) Here's the money. (*She hands him coins*)
Alan (*protesting*) Yes, but . . .
Smith (*pointedly*) That shop closes sharp at half-past seven; sometimes a few minutes before.

Alan glares at Smith. Margaret puts a hand on his arm

Alan (*after a moment, muttering as he goes*) Twenty Embassy . . .
Smith *Plain.*

Alan stops, turns and looks at Smith for a moment, then goes off L

Margaret moves to a light chair, brings it down stage a little and sits on it—half turned away from Smith

(*After a slight pause*) Not a bad-lookin' feller, that Alan. Bit cocky, mind, but, of course—(*eyes well on Margaret*)—he's only a kid yet, isn't 'e? Quite a kid.
Margaret (*suddenly turning to face him*) Mr—er . . . ?
Smith (*laconically*) Smith—Ted Smith.
Margaret (*hesitantly*) Er—when you put the lights on in the hall just now . . . (*She pauses*)
Smith Yes?
Margaret You must have seen—er—Mr Wilson and me—well, more or less in each other's arms.
Smith Not bein' blind, I did.
Margaret (*with a little false laugh*) Well—I hope you didn't get a—a wrong impression.
Smith (*quietly*) No, I don't think so.
Margaret (*after a look at him*) You see—just before you put the lights on, I—I'd had rather a bad scare.
Smith (*laconically*) Oh?
Margaret (*after another look*) Yes, you see—when I came into the hall—I didn't know anyone else was here—I thought I was alone. Then—Mr Wilson suddenly jumped out from—from nowhere, and grabbed me.
Smith (*muttering*) Damn' silly thing to do.
Margaret Of course it was, but—these youngsters—they don't think. But —I was so scared.
Smith I expect you thought it was The Prowler who'd got you?
Margaret The . . . ?
Smith You must've read about him in the local paper? This chap who's goin' round the town at night, attacking young girls.
Margaret Oh, yes, of course. (*With a little laugh*) No, I didn't think it was him, but—I was terribly scared. When Alan—Mr Wilson, realized just how much he'd scared me, he was very upset, and—I suppose it was— instinctive—he put his arms round me.
Smith (*again laconically*) 'Course. Natural, you might say.
Margaret And it was just as he put his arms round me that you—you put the lights on.
Smith (*with a derisive little laugh*) Yeh! I see!

A door is heard to open and slam closed off L

Margaret (*hurriedly*) Look! I don't want any of the others to know—so please . . .

Smith (*almost overlapping; with a meaning laugh*) No, I'll bet you don't.

Smith exits R

Margaret (*again blazing; under her breath*) You . . .!

Philip Stephens, a big, somewhat overpowering man of forty, wearing an overcoat, also a hat at a somewhat rakish angle, comes on from up L. *He is carrying a script, a book or two, and a writing pad*

(*Half surprised, half apprehensive*) Oh! Philip . . .!
Philip (*seeing her*) Good God! You here already? (*Then fairly brusquely*) Here, hold these.
Maigaret What . . . ?

Philip thrusts his script, etc., into Margaret's hands, then at once "gets busy". *He takes his overcoat off and throws it carelessly and untidily on to the chair which Margaret brought down. He tilts his hat back on his head, then moves up stage and takes a whist table from the back wall, brings it down to the proscenium arch, and sets it up*

(*During this; quietly*) Did you get through everything you had to do?
Philip (*gruffly*) What're you talking about?
Margaret (*after a slight pause*) You rang at lunch time to say you wouldn't be home for a meal; that you'd be kept at the office and would come straight here to rehearsal. Remember?
Philip Of course I remember. What the hell are you getting at?

Smith comes on stage from R *slowly. He has a coil of electric wiring in his hand*

Margaret I merely asked you if you got through all you had to do.
Philip I *had* to get through it. (*He points a stabbing finger at the script, etc., which Margaret is holding, then stabs the table, indicating she is to put the things down on it. He moves away from the table*)

Margaret, after a look at Philip, puts the things on the table. Philip takes out his cigarette case, lights a cigarette with a match, then throws the match down on to the stage

Nobody else here yet?
Margaret (*hesitantly*) Er—Alan Wilson's arrived. He's just . . .

Smith moves down to Philip's side

Smith (*pointedly*) 'Scuse me.
Philip (*turning and finding Smith at his side*) What . . . ? Who are you?
Smith I'm the new caretaker here; started last Monday.
Philip (*with a little grunt*) Oh! Well, what's biting you?
Smith (*pointing to it*) That matchstick—would you mind picking it up?
Philip What?

Smith does not speak—just stands looking at Philip

(*Blustering*) Who the hell do you think *you* are to . . . ?

Smith (*cutting in quietly*) I've told you who I am; I'm the caretaker here, an' it's my job to see this 'all doesn't go up in flames, so—(*indicating the matchstick*)—d'y'mind?

Philip Now look here . . . !

Smith (*cutting in*) And there's a biscuit tin either side there—(*indicating the sides of the stage*)—for matches an' fag ends and all suchlike rubbish.

Philip (*fuming*) Then why don't you stuff yourself in one of 'em?

Margaret (*quickly*) Philip!

Philip moves to the chairs at the back and brings one down to behind the table. He makes a pretence of arranging things on the table

Smith (*pointing to the matchstick; truculently*) What about this?

Margaret moves quickly, picks up the matchstick, and moving to the side of the stage, picks up an (unseen) biscuit tin and, after putting the matchstick into it, places it beside the table on the floor

Philip (*looking up from reading; to Margaret*) What are you . . . ? (*Then, seeing the tin, in a sudden burst of temper*) Get that damn thing away from here! (*He kicks the tin viciously up* L)

As Philip kicks the tin, Ronnie Meadows appears up L. *He is a cheerful, tubby little man between forty and fifty. He carries a briefcase*

Ronnie (*as the tin almost lands at his feet—at once*) Right! Give the half-back a chance! (*He dribbles the tin across to* R, *then kicks it off stage*) Goal! Come and kiss me, somebody.

Philip (*his eyes still on Smith; curtly*) Cut it out, Ronnie!

Ronnie Eh?

Philip (*ignoring him; to Smith*) You—you're a new broom here, you say?

Smith So what?

Ronnie (*alert, but speaking brightly*) Hello, hello, hello! What . . . ?

Philip (*to Smith*) Well, don't start sweeping too bloody clean. Play it down a bit or you might find yourself out on your arse.

Margaret (*sharply*) Philip!

Ronnie (*still alert, but brightly*) Ladies present, old boy!

Philip (*ignoring him*) Your boss—the Vicar—we're good friends, and if I . . .

Smith (*quietly*) Talk the same kind of language, I expect.

Philip (*about to go for Smith*) Why you . . . !

As Philip moves to him, Smith raises the coil of wire threateningly

Ronnie (*coming between them; "cheerfully"*) Hey! Hey! Hey! Break it up! Break it up! "All good pals and jolly good compan-ee", eh?

Philip (*after glaring at Smith; speaking generally*) Let me know when that —(*indicating Smith*)—So-and-so is off this stage and then we'll get on with the rehearsal.

Philip storms off up R

Margaret (*pleadingly, in lowered voice*) Ronnie—go after him—calm him down!

Ronnie (*smiling at her*) Hey! I'm the stage manager of this Society, not the ruddy lion-tamer! (*As he goes off* L) Now where's that naughty Philip? (*He has taken his briefcase with him*)

Ronnie exits

There is an awkward pause. Smith is making a pretence of examining the coil of wire

Margaret (*at last*) I—I'm sorry my husband was so—so . . .

Alan Wilson returns quickly from up L. *He has a twenty packet of cigarettes in his hand. He stops on seeing Smith*

Smith (*meanwhile*) Your—husband, eh?
Margaret (*quietly*) Yes.
Smith Thought so from the way he talked to you. Young Alan was right, wasn't he, when he said he was a bit on the bombastic side?

Margaret and Alan both react

Margaret (*almost desperately*) Alan, did you get the . . . ?
Alan (*with his eyes on Smith*) Yes. (*He hands the packet to Margaret*)
Margaret Bless you. (*She quickly strips the Cellophane and opens the packet. Moving to Smith*) Would you—(*she tips the packet so that a cigarette is protruding*)—care for . . . ?
Smith (*with a thin smile, taking a cigarette*) Ta! These are more in my line.
Margaret Light? (*She takes a lighter from her bag and flicks it*)

Smith, with no word of thanks, lights his cigarette from the lighter which Margaret is holding out

Smith (*after drawing on the cigarette and exhaling smoke*) Damn! (*To Alan*) Why didn't I ask you to get *me* a packet while you were at it?
Margaret (*in a controlled voice*) You can—take these if you're—short.
Smith (*with feigned surprise*) Oh! Oh well! (*Taking the packet*) Thanks. Thanks very much. (*Not putting his hand in his pocket*) Now, let's see. How much are they now?
Margaret (*still controlled*) Please—don't bother about . . .
Smith (*with the thin smile again*) You're very kind. Thanks a lot. Well, if you'll excuse me. I've got one or two jobs to see to. (*He looks at Margaret, then Alan, smiling*) Be seein' you.

Smith moves to the steps leading to the auditorium, and after throwing the coil down on stage by the table, descends the steps and disappears at the back of the hall

Alan (*when Smith is half-way down the hall; under his breath*) I'd like to kill that swine!
Margaret (*putting a hand on his arm; quietly*) Sssh!

A door at the back of the auditorium slams as Smith exits

Alan (*turning to Margaret and taking her by the arms; eagerly*) Margaret . . .
Margaret (*stepping back; urgently*) For God's sake . . . !
Alan (*pulling up*) What . . . ?
Margaret (*in a low voice, urgently*) Be careful. Mind what you say. Philip —he's up in the men's dressing-room.
Alan But—that caretaker chap. You shouldn't have played up to him. I mean—giving him those cigarettes. It was blackmail; nothing more or less.
Margaret It certainly wasn't generosity on my part. (*Moving*) Damn the man!
Alan D'you think we're going to have trouble with him?
Margaret Of course we are. You heard what he said about Philip being bombastic. He obviously heard every word we said—before he put the house lights up.
Alan If he *does* make trouble, I'll break his neck.
Margaret Don't talk nonsense.
Alan But what *can* we do?
Margaret For one thing, we can stop all this right now.
Alan Stop what?
Margaret (*almost sharply*) Don't be so naive; you know what. I must have been mad to ever let it start.

A door is heard to open up R

Look out!
Alan (*after a quick look* R) But—Margaret . . . (*He moves towards her*)
Margaret (*quickly as she moves a step back; still in a low voice*) No! Stay where you are. (*She looks* R) And—don't say anything—stupid.
Alan (*quickly, hurt*) Stupid?
Margaret (*with slight exasperation*) You know what I mean. Talk about —ordinary things. (*Again the look* R) Philip may be back any moment, and Ronnie's here—and the others will soon . . .
Alan (*desperately*) But—when am I going to see you again—alone?
Margaret (*in a low voice, but almost angrily*) Alan . . . !
Alan I've got to see you, Margaret. You don't know what hell it is for me when I don't see you—if only for ten minutes. I . . .
Margaret (*tensely, under her breath*) It's got to stop, I tell you. We've both got to pull ourselves together, d'you hear?
Alan You mean you . . . ?

The door off L *slams again*

Margaret (*at once, in a slightly artificial "ordinary" voice*) I had intended knowing my first act—(*she takes a script from her bag*)—but instead of studying last night I got stuck in front of the telly, and . . .

Phoebe Kershaw, a plumpish, slightly masculine-looking woman of fifty enters L. She is carrying a handbag, a bottle of milk, a shopping basket and an umbrella. She is shrewd but pleasant-natured

(*Breaking off; brightly*) 'Lo, Phoebe!

Phoebe 'Lo, Margaret. I thought *I'd* be first!

Margaret No. Philip and Ronnie are here, and—(*indicating him*)—Alan.

Phoebe 'Lo. Alan. Didn't see you there. (*After a quick look at him*) What's the matter?

Alan (*almost surly*) Matter? Nothing. Why?

Phoebe (*with a shrug*) Just thought you looked a bit down in the mouth. (*She gives a quick look towards Margaret*)

Margaret, aware of the look, looks away

(*To Alan*) Look! Be a lamb, will you, and put this down in the kitchen for me? (*She holds out a bottle of milk*) It is my turn to do the coffee tonight, isn't it?

Margaret I don't know, darling. I know I did them last week.

Phoebe Yes, I'm sure it is. (*To Alan again*) Oh, and would you mind turning the hot water thing on for me. Scares me to death to go near it. It ought to be seen to. You don't mind, do you?

Alan No. (*He moves R*)

Phoebe Thank you, dear. (*With a smile*) Don't electrocute yourself with the boiler, will you?

Alan (*gloomily*) Why not?

Alan, after a quick look towards Margaret, goes off L

Phoebe has noticed the look. Margaret, aware of this, moves slightly, with her back to Phoebe

Phoebe (*quietly*) He's a bit sorry for himself tonight, isn't he?

Margaret (*with a slightly overdone casual tone*) Alan? Is he? I hadn't noticed.

Phoebe looks towards Margaret's back for a moment, then moves up to the form, puts her bag, etc., down on it, then removes the capacious cape she is wearing

Phoebe (*as she does this*) How's that husband of yours?

Margaret (*turning*) How do you mean—how is he?

Phoebe What sort of a mood is he in tonight? He was in a hellish one last Friday.

Margaret Well—you know what it's like—when you're—*producing* a play.

Phoebe No, I don't. I've never produced a play. (*With a grin*) 'Spect some people would say I'd never *acted* in one either.

Margaret (*smiling*) Now then! No false modesty. You know you make the rest of us look even more amateurish than we really are. (*Slight pause*) How long were you a professional, Phoebe?

Phoebe (*after a slight pause*) Long enough to realize I'd never get anywhere.

Margaret I don't believe that. You're a terrific actress. Marvellous in any part you tackle.

Phoebe I'm going to be ruddy awful in this one, let me tell you.

Margaret Rubbish!

Phoebe (*skimming through the pages*) What a load of tripe! I know it's a rule in the Society that producers can choose the play they want to do, but why Philip picked on this opus I'll never know.

Margaret (*with a shrug of the shoulders*) You know how keen he is on thrillers, and I expect it'll go like a bomb. You know how our audiences love to puzzle their brains over who-dunnits.

Phoebe (*holding out the typescript*) As far as *this* is concerned, the only thing that'll puzzle 'em is *why* we did it. (*Throwing the script down disgustedly*) What a pain in the neck!

Ronnie enters up R

Ronnie (*brightly*) Who's a pain in the neck?

Phoebe (*grinning*) You are usually; but I'm talking about this play.

Ronnie Well, for God's sake, don't! At least not in front of Philip. He's touchy about it enough as it is.

Margaret Where is Philip? Is he coming down?

Ronnie (*moving up to the chairs at the back*) He's just slipped over to . . . (*He pulls up short. Embarrassed*) I don't suppose he'll be long.

Margaret looks quickly at Ronnie, as does Phoebe, who then looks towards Margaret

(*Lamely*) It's only just on half past, anyway. (*Embarrassed*) I'll get the stage set. (*He begins to bring chairs and a couple of tables down, and sets them out in the required position for rehearsal*)

Meanwhile, Margaret has half turned away from the others. She is obviously troubled. She takes a cigarette from her bag, lights it and stands quite still as she smokes. Ronnie and Phoebe are very much "aware" of Margaret. They look towards her and significantly at each other from time to time. After a little "setting", Ronnie moves to the table, picks up Philip's script and consults it

Now let's see. (*Reading*) "Settee by fireplace, Right." (*Looking at the chairs*) Yes. Got that. (*Script again*) "Armchair, Left Centre." (*He adjusts an "armchair" a little*)

Phoebe (*reading from her script*) "Table by armchair, Left Centre."

Ronnie (*grinning*) Know-all!

Phoebe (*lightly*) Only trying to help.

Ronnie You're too kind. (*He puts a whist table* L *of the armchair*)

Margaret suddenly pulls herself together and turns to the others

Margaret I—I—I'll just . . .

Margaret goes quickly off L

The unseen door off L *is heard to open and slam. Again—without speaking—
Phoebe and Ronnie look at each other significantly. Then Phoebe sings quietly,
but somewhat pointedly, to herself. During this, Ronnie gets a whist table
and sets it up by the proscenium* L

Phoebe (*singing*)
    "Nobody knows the trouble I see
    Nobody knows the trouble I see
    Nobody knows the trouble I see
    Nobody knows like . . ."
Ronnie (*with a grin*) O.K.! O.K.! You've made your point. Thank God
    I'm a bachelor. At least . . .
Phoebe He *has* gone across to the pub, I take it?
Ronnie Philip? Yes. (*He brings a chair to behind the table down* L)
Phoebe And she's gone to fetch him out. Oh Lordy, Lordy! That'll please
    him I *don't* think. He behaved himself quite well during the last show,
    didn't he?
Ronnie Yes.
Phoebe 'Course he wasn't *producing* that one—just playing in it. Hardly
    blame him if he does go off the rails a bit now. This play's enough to
    drive anyone to drink.
Ronnie (*looking round*) Now where did I leave my . . .
Phoebe What? Your aspirin? Better find 'em. You're going to need 'em
    tonight, comrade.
Ronnie (*absently*) Oh, shut up! My *briefcase*—I had it when I . . . Oh, I
    know! I took it upstairs with me.

Ronnie exits R

*Phoebe sits on a form, almost with her back to the audience and, humming
"Nobody knows" to herself, begins turning things out of her basket, obviously
searching for something*

   *During this, Smith comes through the auditorium and up on to the stage.
   Phoebe's back is towards him. Taking no notice of Phoebe, Smith is
   moving towards up* L *when Phoebe happens to notice him*

Phoebe (*with a big start, as she recognizes him*) Oh! (*She rises quickly*)

*Smith turns. He too gives a start when he recognizes Phoebe. They just stare
at each other for a while*

   (*In an almost horrified whisper*) Smith!

Smith is silent

   (*Quietly but accusingly*) You are—Smith—aren't you?

Smith is silent

   (*Putting a hand to her head. She is obviously very distressed*) Oh—God!

Smith (*moving forward*) 'Ere! You're not goin' to faint, are you?
Phoebe (*suddenly, flaring*) Keep away from me! (*Quieter*) Don't you dare
   touch me!
Smith (*halted*) Now—look . . . (*His voice tails away*)
Phoebe (*after a slight pause, with hatred in her voice*) What are you doing
   here?
Smith (*muttering*) I'm the caretaker; just got the job.

Phoebe can only stare at him for a while

Phoebe (*at last, slowly and in almost a whisper*) Get out of my sight!
Smith (*almost whining*) Look—it was ten years ago now. You're not going
   to . . .
Phoebe Ten years—twenty years—as long as I live—I'll never forget,
   Smith. And I've always sworn that if ever I got the chance to do you an
   injury . . . (*Near to tears*) For God's sake get out of my sight.

Smith after a long look at Phoebe goes off L

*Phoebe stands quite still for a moment, then, after dabbing her eyes im-
patiently with a handkerchief, pulls herself together, and begins turning her
bag out again*

*After quite a long pause Patricia Robins, who has presumably come through
the front of the hall, appears at the foot of the steps leading to the stage.
She hesitates a moment on the bottom step. Patricia (Pat) is a pretty girl
of twenty, quiet but intelligent*

Pat (*in a somewhat subdued voice*) Hello, Phoebe!

Phoebe spins round

Phoebe Who . . . ? (*Then seeing Pat, at once her old cheerful self*) Oh! It's
   you, Pat. How's life?

Pat comes up on to the stage

Pat (*smiling, as she looks at things from Phoebe's basket*) Having a good
   old turn-out, aren't you?
Phoebe I'm searching for my front door key. Damned if I know where it is.
   (*She continues searching*)
Pat (*smiling*) Probably in your front door.
Phoebe (*with mock drama*) Oh, Gawd! I hope not.
Pat Perhaps when you get home tonight, you'll find a very attractive man
   sitting in your armchair.
Phoebe If he is, he'll damn' soon get out of it.
Pat You wouldn't like that?
Phoebe I would not. Neither would he by the time I'd finished with him.
Pat Aren't you—scared, living completely on your own?
Phoebe Scared? Why should I be?
Pat *I* should be. Specially just now—with this—"Prowler" fellow loose
   on the town.

Phoebe (*with a little laugh*) I don't think *I* need worry about *him*. He can't be so desperate that he'd bother to chase an old bird like me. I should say you're more his type. You're the one to be careful, duckie.

Pat I *am*—or rather my mother is; wouldn't let me walk to rehearsal tonight; she made my brother bring me in his car.

Phoebe (*suddenly, with anger*) The bastard!

Pat (*smiling*) You're not referring to my brother, I hope!

Phoebe Don't be stupid. This prowler bloke. I suppose the police *will* get him—eventually. And it might be an awful shock to a lot of folk when they do.

Pat How do you mean, Phoebe?

Phoebe Nobody knows who he is—not yet—do they? He might turn out to be one of the town's most respected citizens. Well—if he did! Or, suppose, it was someone *we* know?

Pat (*smiling*) You're just trying to scare the life out of me, aren't you?

Phoebe (*also smiling*) Am I?

Pat (*changing the subject*) Who—who was the man on the stage just now; the one you were talking to when I came in—(*nodding her head*)—through the front?

Phoebe (*sharply*) Why?

Pat (*surprised*) What?

Phoebe (*almost flustered*) He—he's the new caretaker of this place.

Pat (*after a curious look at Phoebe*) Oh! Thought I hadn't seen him around before. (*Then, after taking the script from her bag*) Isn't it time this rehearsal got on its way? Where is everybody?

Phoebe Here and there; those that *are* here.

Pat (*removing her coat*) Alan—is he . . . ?

Phoebe (*with a look at her, grinning*) Oh, yes; don't worry. Alan's here.

Pat "Worry"? Why should *I* worry?

Phoebe Come off it! I'm not blind, child. You're nuts about him.

Pat (*in dismay*) Oh, Phoebe—does it show as badly as that?

Phoebe (*calmly*) It does.

Pat (*putting her coat down on a chair*) And I don't believe he's really aware of my existence.

Phoebe (*quietly*) No, not at the moment. He has—(*she gives a little cough*)—other—er—fish to fry or thinks he has.

Pat Meaning . . . ?

Phoebe (*with a big false smile*) Sweet damn-all, duckie—as usual.

Pat (*smiling*) You're a wicked old So-and-so.

Ronnie, briefcase in hand, comes in R

Ronnie Hya, Pat!

Pat Oh, Ronnie, I wanted to ask you . . .

Ronnie (*genially, moving to the prompt table*) In a minute, love. Things are a bit hectic at the moment . . .

Pat But . . .

Ronnie (*grinning*) Don't worry, Pat. I love you very much! (*He quickly* *kisses her brow, then speaks to Phoebe*) They're not back yet, are they, Phoebe?

Phoebe Ask a silly question and you'll get a silly answer.

Pat Who's not back?

Alan enters up R

(*Seeing him*) Oh!

Phoebe (*answering Pat's question*) Philip and Margaret. They . . . (*Seeing that Pat is not listening. Grinning*) That's right, Phoebe, old girl; talk to yourself.

Pat (*with warmth*) Hello, Alan.

Alan (*vaguely*) 'Lo, Pat. (*He moves unconsciously to the "producer's" chair and sprawls in it, lost in unhappy thought*)

Pat watches him for a moment, then moves to Ronnie at his table

Pat Ronnie . . .

Ronnie (*grinning*) There's no satisfying the woman; sex-starved, that's what's the matter with her! (*He again kisses her on the brow*)

Pat Ronnie do be serious a minute.

Ronnie (*after drawing his hand over his grinning face and revealing a "cod serious" one*) I'm serious.

Pat (*laughing*) You fool! Will you be going straight home tonight after rehearsal?

Ronnie (*somewhat shaken*) Will I . . . ?

Pat It doesn't really matter if you're not, but . . .

Ronnie I shudder to think what's coming!

Pat If you *are*, can I come with you as . . .

Ronnie My God! She wants to seduce me! (*To the others*) You all heard! You're my witnesses!

Pat (*laughing*) Ronnie, I'll clock you one in a minute. It's just that Mum's scared about this "Prowler" fellow, and as you have to pass our house on your way home . . .

Ronnie Oh, that's your excuse, is it? What about our handsome juvenile over there? (*Indicating Alan*) Wouldn't you rather he . . . ?

Alan (*flustered*) I'm sorry, I have to . . .

Pat (*quickly and embarrassed*) Alan lives in the opposite direction, you clot! (*More embarrassed*) Look! It doesn't matter. I—I'll ask Philip if I can leave early; get the last bus.

Ronnie (*slapping her bottom lightly*) Now don't be silly! Or course I'll see you home—and to hell with what happens to my virginity! (*He is moving the "producer's" table as he says this. He now sees Alan in the chair above it. Grinning*) You producing this play?

Alan (*vaguely*) Eh?

Ronnie (*making pretence of swiping Alan*) Git art of it!

Alan rises and moves away up L

Pat (*who is now near Phoebe*) Where's Philip? Isn't he . . .

The door off L *is heard to open and slam*

Phoebe (*quickly*) Ssssh! This might be him. And watch your step!
Pat What? Why?

> *Philip enters up* L, *quickly, and obviously not too pleased with life. Finding Alan in his way he brushes him aside with one arm, then moves down to his table*

Alan (*as he is brushed aside*) Hey! What . . . ?

Phoebe quickly gives Alan a "shut up" gesture

Philip (*fairly brusquely*) Stage set, Ronnie?
Ronnie Yep!

> *During this, Margaret comes quietly on up* L. *She and Pat exchange silent "Hello's"*

Philip (*standing behind the table, making a pretence of looking at the script*) Right. Everybody here? Time we got cracking. Stand by, beginners, act two.
Ronnie (*seated at his table with his script; automatically*) Stand by, beginners, act two.
Philip (*consulting his script*) Who opens this act?
Ronnie (*unconsciously repeating*) Who opens this act?

Philip glares at Ronnie who is busy with his script

Philip (*brusquely*) Alan, you're on at the beginning, aren't you?
Alan (*vaguely*) Oh, am I?
Philip (*witheringly*) For God's sake!
Ronnie (*automatically*) For God's sake!

Philip again glares at Ronnie

Philip (*to Alan*) You and Doris open this act. (*Looking round*) And where's Doris, dammit? Don't say she hasn't turned up yet?

The others look around somewhat surprised. They had, obviously never thought about the missing Doris

Margaret Oh, yes, of course—Doris!
Ronnie I haven't seen her.
Phoebe Nor have I, and she's usually the first one here.
Philip (*fuming*) My God, this is the limit. I'll have something to say to Miss Doris Stewart when she does get here. (*Consulting his watch*) Look at the time! Nearly ten to eight! Well, we'll carry on without her. Ronnie, you read in for Doris.
Ronnie (*blinking*) Me? (*He rises*)
Philip (*curtly*) You.
Ronnie Oh, girls! (*With one hand on hip, he minces to* C *and back*) I say! This isn't the scene where Doris gets strangled, is it?

Philip (*intent on his script*) It is not.

Ronnie Oh, what a pity! I'd've been marvellous—being strangled! (*He puts both hands around his own throat and, staggering, makes very phoney "strangling" noises*)

All, except Philip, are amused at his performance. Ronnie, doing his "strangling" act, has moved nearer Philip, unconsciously. He slowly becomes aware of Philip's icy stare. The "strangling" noises fade away. He removes his hands from his neck

(*Mumbling*) Sorry!

Philip (*coldly*) Ronnie . . .

Ronnie Yes, old man?

Philip Try to forget everyone thinks you're a comic.

Ronnie (*trying to be indignant*) Oh, I say, look here . . . !

Philip Right! With Ronnie's permission—we'll get started, shall we? Stand by, everyone!

Ronnie moves to his table

At the same time Smith comes on down L and begins to cross up R

Philip sees this and moves up to R of Smith, thus preventing him from going farther

(*Angrily*) And what the devil do you think *you're* doing?

Smith (*truculently*) *Now* what's up?

Philip What do you mean by barging on to the stage when there's a rehearsal on?

Smith (*with belligerence*) Now, look here, Mister . . . !

Philip I'll look no damn where! But you'll get yourself off this stage—and quick—or I'll bloody well throw you off!

Smith (*shouting loudly*) I'm the caretaker 'ere! I've got my work to do.

Philip (*grabbing Smith near the throat with one hand, and speaking quieter, but threateningly*) Listen to me, you little rat! You may be the caretaker here, but you'd better get it firmly into your head that we *hire this hall*; we pay good money to use the place, and while we're *in* it, it belongs to us. Get that? (*He almost throws Smith off*)

Smith (*muttering*) I'll see the Vicar about this, you see if I don't! He's given me my instructions and I'm goin' to carry 'em out and—(*glaring at Philip*)—just you, or anybody else, try to stop me!

Smith goes off up R

The assembled Company all look somewhat embarrassed, except Phoebe who is looking R, where Smith went off

Phoebe (*suddenly moving to Philip, grabbing him by the arm, and speaking intensely, and with a note of hysteria in her voice*) You've got to get that man out of here; you've *got* to!

Everyone—even Philip—is taken aback by Phoebe's little outburst. Phoebe,
aware of everyone's amazement, is very embarrassed

(*Almost smiling*) I'm sorry. It was silly of me, but that man . . . (*She gives*
a little shudder, then deliberately pulls herself together. She then speaks
in a somewhat overdone bright tone) Sorry for the melodrama, folks!

The tension is eased somewhat. Philip moves down to his table. He stands
quite still for a moment, then, after running his hand, almost wearily, across
his brow, turns to face the company

Philip (*in a low, dejected voice*) Let's get on for *God's* sake.
Ronnie (*automatically*) Let's get on for God's sake.
Philip (*to Ronnie, exasperated*) Well, *get* on!
Ronnie (*blinking*) Eh?
Philip (*patiently*) You're reading for Doris. She's playing "Freda" and she
begins this act.

The others sit at the back of the stage, out of the scene

Ronnie (*leaping up and almost upsetting the table, picking up the script*)
Oh, sorry! Now where . . . ?
Philip (*looking at his own script*) She's reclining on the settee when the
curtain rises.
Ronnie (*moving towards the very small form representing the settee*) Reclining on the . . . (*He blinks at the form*) Er—(*to Philip*)—d'you want *me*
to—recline on that?

Philip, occupied with his script, ignores him

Oh! Oh well—(*he, very gingerly, lies full length on his back on the form*)
—I'm reclining! (*Then in sudden fright*) Whoops! (*He drops his script on*
his ample stomach and grabs the sides of the form frantically)

Philip is not watching Ronnie. As Ronnie grabs the sides of the form, his
script falls off his stomach to the floor—up stage side. He wildly tries to save
it, and promptly falls off the form up stage. The rest of the cast (except
Philip) try to control their laughter—very much aware of Philip—but are
unable to do so

(*His face just appearing above the form; apprehensively*) Sorry! (*He is*
again about to recline)
Philip (*in an obviously controlled voice*) Just *sit* on the ruddy thing!
Ronnie Oh! Oh, yes! (*He sits on the form with his back to the audience*)
Philip The *other* way round, d'you mind?
Ronnie (*in a state of dither*) Oh! Oh, yes, of course! (*He swings over to face*
the audience)
Philip (*still in a controlled voice though inwardly seething*) Sit at the end of
the settee.
Ronnie Oh! Oh, yes! Er—which end?
Philip Left.

Ronnie "Left." Right! (*He slides to the* R *end of the form, which—under his weight—begins to tip up*) Whoops! (*He controls the form, then looks at Philip, mumbling*) Sorry!

Philip (*scathingly*) Any more funny business you want to get out of your system before we continue? If so, don't mind us; we'll wait.

Ronnie (*mumbling*) Sorry!

Philip (*by his table, script in hand; suddenly calling*) Peter!

Philip is calling to Alan, who is gazing unhappily towards Margaret, who is concentrating on her script

Phoebe (*trying to draw Alan's attention to Philip*) Alan!

Philip (*annoyed*) Peter! (*Then barking*) Alan!

Alan (*with a start*) Oh! What . . . ?

Philip Your entrance!

Alan (*distrait*) Oh, yes, of course. I'm "Peter", aren't I?

Philip (*sourly*) You are, and it's your entrance.

Alan (*fumbling with his script*) Er—where do I come on from?

Philip You're "Peter", but you're not Peter Pan, so you don't fly in through the ruddy window. You come through the door up left.

Alan Oh, yes, of course. (*Moving up* L) Door up left.

Philip And you're heard calling off before your entrance.

Alan O.K. Ready?

Philip I've been ready *and* waiting for the last five minutes.

Alan (*mumbling*) Sorry! (*Reading from his script*) Freda! Freda! Where are you?

Ronnie (*reading from his script, in a high falsetto voice*) I'm here, darling!

The rest of the cast giggle somewhat

Philip (*glaring at Ronnie*) Your own voice will do!

Ronnie (*mumbling*) Sorry! (*In his own voice*) "I'm here, darling!" (*To Philip*) That better?

Philip (*ignoring Ronnie*) That's your entrance, Peter.

Alan makes an "entrance"

Alan (*script*) "Oh, there you are!"

Ronnie (*script*) "Yes, darling."

Philip (*to Alan*) You sit beside her on the settee, left of her.

Alan Oh, yes, of course. (*He moves* L *of the form. To Ronnie*) Oi!

Ronnie What?

Alan Move up a bit!

Ronnie slides to the R *end of the form. It tilts again*

Ronnie Whoops!

Ronnie looks guiltily at Philip who is glaring at him. Alan sits gingerly at the extreme L *end of the form*

Philip (*heavily*) Carry on!

Ronnie (*script*) "Darling, you look worried. There's nothing wrong is there?"

Alan (*script*) "No, nothing. Nothing at all."

Ronnie (*script*) "Peter, you're not telling me the truth. There *is* something troubling you. I can see it in your eyes."

Alan, during Ronnie's last speech, is looking towards Margaret

(*Nudging him*) Oi!

Alan (*turning*) What . . . ?

Ronnie Look at me.

Alan What . . . ?

Ronnie If you don't look at me how can I see it in your eyes?

Alan See what?

Ronnie Gawd knows, old boy, but it says here—(*script*)—that I can see it in your eyes, whatever it is.

Philip (*cuttingly*) When you've quite finished . . .

Ronnie But . . .

Philip For heaven's sake, carry on!

Ronnie (*after a resigned shrug of the shoulders; to Alan*) It's you.

Alan No, it isn't. It's you.

Ronnie It isn't. I've just said . . .

Philip (*raising his voice*) Don't let's have a ruddy inquest about it. Ronnie, go back to your line "There is something troubling you."

Alan is looking at the script. Ronnie, using both hands, turns Alan's face so he can look into his eyes

Ronnie (*looking into Alan's eyes*) "There is something troubling you. I can see it in your eyes."

Alan (*script*) "Freda . . ."

Ronnie (*script*) "But you never tell me anything these days; not even that you . . ." (*Taking Alan's hand in his*)

Alan and Ronnie giggle, then, aware of Philip's glare, sober up

Alan (*script*) "Not even that I what?"

Ronnie (*script*) "Not even that you—(*he slides along the form, closer to Alan, and gazes at him "adoringly" and speaks in a husky "passionate" voice*)—that you love me!" (*His face is close to Alan's*)

Alan (*bending backwards to get away from him. Script*) "Freda . . ."

Ronnie (*moving suddenly closer still to Alan*) "Peter . . ."

The inevitable happens. The form tips up and both Ronnie and Alan land on the floor. The others on stage (with the exception of Philip) laugh loudly

Philip (*flinging his script on the table*) Damn and blast you, Ronnie! (*To the others*) Shut up all of you!

Ronnie (*picking himself up*) Sorry, but I got carried away!

Margaret gives an involuntary snort of laughter

Philip (*to Margaret, suddenly losing complete control*) And what the hell's the matter with you?

Margaret (*stung*) Philip!
Philip I never did rate your sense of humour very high, but if you think Ronnie's pathetic cracks are funny, well . . .
Ronnie Oh, now look . . .
Philip (*snapping at him*) I'm talking to my wife.
Margaret (*also snapping*) I wish you'd remember that!
Philip What? Why . . . !

Alan, forgetting he is sitting on the floor, and desperately anxious to prevent further altercations between Philip and Margaret suddenly shouts his next line from the play

Alan (*in a loud, unnatural voice*) "I love you. I shall love you till the day I die."

Everyone looks at Alan as if he had gone mad. Aware of their looks, he shows great embarrassment

Philip What . . . ?
Alan (*almost mumbling*) Er—that's my next line.
Philip Is it?
Alan (*miserably*) Yes.
Philip And do you bawl it out at the top of your voice from the floor?
Alan Oh—I . . . (*He gets to his feet*)
Philip (*fuming*) Ronnie, you must have exhausted your repertoire of funny business with this thing—(*indicating the form*)—by now, so we'll get rid of it and use three chairs instead. Bring three chairs down, somebody.
Ronnie I'll get 'em. (*He moves up to the chairs at the back, gets two and brings them down to near the form*)
Philip (*indicating the form*) And get rid of that—(*heavily*)—if you can bear to part with it.

Ronnie picks up the form and takes it up stage

(*Meanwhile*) And listen, everybody! I've had all the fooling I can take for one evening—(*suddenly barking*)—you listening, Ronnie?

Ronnie is now slightly down C with the third chair in his hand)

Ronnie (*mumbling*) Yes.
Philip (*speaking generally*) I know that most of you have no time for this play; that you think it's just a commercial run-of-the-mill who-dunnit. And what's wrong with that, for God's sake? Isn't it the sort of play our audiences want—what they pay good money to see? They certainly don't want the other stuff! Look how much we lose when we try to give 'em the classics or these way-out plays! They stay away in droves—and I for one, don't blame 'em. There's too much damned nonsense talked about educating the public. They don't *want* us to educate them—and why the hell should they? All they want us to do is *entertain* them.
Ronnie With *this* play?

Philip (*turning on him*) Yes, with *this* play. I'll lay you an even fiver that it goes like a bomb—*and* that we make money with it. (*Then, speaking generally again*) And there's something else you might all bear in mind. Beggars can't be chosers. Our acting strength has never been as low as it is just now. We're just not getting new members—don't ask me why—and those we *have* got—well, the only thing to be said in their favour is, they've paid their subscriptions! So, at the moment, until we've licked the newcomers into some sort of shape, we've *got* to find small cast plays. That isn't easy.

Phoebe (*with a quick glance at the script in her hand*) Obviously!

Philip (*raising his voice a little*) This was the best of . . .

There is a sudden, prolonged noise just off R, as of several fairly heavy objects falling to the floor

What the . . . ?

Pat from where she is sitting can see off R

Pat (*almost apprehensively*) It's—it's the caretaker. He's emptying a cupboard or something.

Philip (*moving up R, fuming; almost overlapping Pat's speech*) I'll break his blasted neck if . . . (*Shouting off R*) What the devil are you . . . ?

A few more crashes are heard

(*Louder*) Hey, *you*!

Ronnie (*grinning*) Take cover, everybody!

Smith almost strolls on up R

Philip What do you think you're . . . ?

Smith holds up in both hands, and exhibits, a pair of very old-fashioned red bloomers

Smith (*to Philip, laconically*) These yours?

There is a burst of laughter from everyone except Philip and Phoebe

Philip (*almost speechless with rage*) You—you . . . !

Smith (*after showing "appreciation" of the laughter he has caused*) I mean —do they belong to your Society?

Philip moves down to his table, incapable of speech. He stands beating a clenched fist on the table top

Y'see, I'm turning out a cupboard out there and I come across 'em. An' *I* don't know who they belong to.

Alan (*being "funny"*) P'raps they're the Vicar's!

Subdued laughter at Alan's crack, except from Philip, Margaret and Phoebe

Margaret (*with her eyes on Philip; almost viciously to Alan*) Shut up, Alan!

Alan (*stung by Margaret's tone*) I'm sorry. I only . . . !

Ronnie (*very brightly*) *Wait* a minute! *I* know whose they are! (*Grinning*) Phoebe, darling . . . ?

Phoebe (*fairly curtly*) Yes?

Ronnie Remember last week, you and I stayed on a bit after the others had gone, and when we were leaving I *asked* if you'd remembered to put 'em on again?

Yelps of laughter from all but Philip and Phoebe

Philip (*suddenly turning and shouting*) Shut up! *Shut up* the lot of you!

Dead silence

(*In a more subdued, but tense voice; to Smith*) And you—(*approaching him*)—you get off this stage d'you hear, and—(*suddenly snatching the bloomers from Smith and hurling them off up* L)—take these bloody things with you.

Smith, somewhat cowed, turns to go

A door slams off up L, *and stumbling footsteps are heard approaching. A chair is heard to overturn, then Doris Stewart almost staggers on* L. *She supports herself against a chair. Doris is a young woman of twenty-five, normally quite self-possessed, but now obviously in a distressed state. Her hair and clothing are dishevelled. She is bare-headed*

Margaret (*loudly*) Doris! What . . . ?

There is vocal amazement from the others. All, except Philip and Smith crowd round Doris, firing questions at her. Philip moves down to his table in exasperation. Smith, just stands looking across towards Doris

Phoebe (*as the hubbub subsides*) Doris, what's happened?

Ronnie She looks as if she's going to . . . Shall I go and get some brandy?

Doris (*in a slightly hysterical voice*) No! I'm all right—or I will be when—oh, God!

Margaret (*anxiously*) Let her sit down.

Doris is put into a chair

Doris I'll be all right when . . . (*She pulls herself together somewhat*) I— I've been attacked by . . .

Phoebe (*cutting in*) Not that Prowler swine?

Doris Could have been.

Margaret Oh, God!

Philip and Smith are both listening

Doris I was coming across that bit of waste land—just across the street from here and he—someone—jumped out of the darkness and—grabbed me.

Pat Oh, Doris . . .

Doris I suppose I was lucky, because—while we were struggling—the lights of a car caught us for a moment, and—whoever it was must've got scared 'cos he suddenly let go of me and I fell on the ground—and he ran off.

Margaret But how long ago was this?

Doris What time is it now? I've no idea.

Ronnie Nearly eight.

Doris Then it must've been about an hour ago.

Margaret An *hour*? But . . .

Doris I was on my way here. I intended arriving early so I could run through my lines on my own for a bit.

Phoebe But where have you been all this time?

Doris I—I don't know. Just walking about, I suppose. I don't remember how long for. You see, when I fell, I—I caught my head on a stone, and . . .

Unconsciously, Phoebe's hand goes gently to the back of Doris's head. Immediately, Phoebe gives a little cry of horror, withdrawing her hand quickly. The palm of her hand is covered with blood

Phoebe (*aghast*) Doris!

Exclamations from all

(*Quickly*) Alan—somebody—get some water, quick, and we want . . .

Alan dashes off up L

Smith approaches Phoebe

Smith (*to Phoebe*) There's a first aid box in the cupboard out there. (*He jerks his head towards the exit up* L)

Phoebe (*loudly, sharply*) Keep back, you!

Ronnie (*sharply, to Smith*) Get it!

Smith exits up L

Margaret (*meanwhile*) Doris--did you see the man's face? Would you recognize him if you . . . ?

Phoebe (*authoritatively*) Don't worry her with any more questions just now. We ought to get the police here.

Margaret Yes, of course—right away!

Doris (*suddenly, loudly*) No, Margaret, no!

Margaret What?

Doris Not the police! (*She drags herself to her feet*)

Margaret But . . .

Doris (*quieter; slowly*) Not the . . . (*Her eyes have focused on Philip who is looking across at her from his table*) Not the police—not yet!

The others realize she is looking towards Philip. Their eyes turn on him also, as—

the CURTAIN *falls*

ACT II

The same. Fifteen minutes later

When the CURTAIN *rises, Doris is seated on a chair by Ronnie's table. Phoebe is by her side, securing a roughish bandage round Doris's head with a safety pin. On the table is a small, somewhat grubby, glass bowl. The first aid box is also on the table*

Phoebe How's that feel? Not too tight?
Doris No.
Phoebe It's not too bad a cut; not deep, I mean.
Doris (*with a faint smile*) You mean it won't affect my brains?
Phoebe How can it? You haven't got any.
Doris I *beg* your pardon?
Phoebe If you had, the police would be here right now.
Doris P'raps it's because I *have* brains that they aren't.
Phoebe (*after a look at Doris*) You may—I say "may"—know what you're talking about, but I'm damned if I do.
Doris (*after a look at her*) You wouldn't swear to that, would you, Phoebe, that you don't know what I'm talking about?
Phoebe (*after a slight pause*) No, perhaps not. But—for the moment—the less said, the better.

Ronnie charges on up L

Ronnie (*breezily*) Ah! And how's the patient, Sister?
Phoebe (*with mock asperity*) I thought I told you—the whole lot of you— to go across to the pub and stay there for a bit.
Ronnie (*grinning*) I did stay there for a bit. If I'd stayed there one *bit* longer I'd've come back as tight as a tick!
Phoebe Sure you're not as tight as one now?
Ronnie (*with indignation*) 'Course I'm not.
Phoebe Then why do you *look* as if you are?
Ronnie Here I say . . . And why are you—operating up here? (*He indicates the bowl, first aid box and Doris*)—and on *my* table—if you please! (*Fussing at the table*) If you've soaked my script in water . . . (*He picks up his script, looks at it quickly, gives a yelp*) Aaah!—(*pointing to a page of his script, which has a red stain on it; in mock horror*)—what's that—that red stuff?
Phoebe (*cryptically*) Blood!
Doris (*likewise*) Mine. (*She rises*)

Phoebe tries to stop Doris rising

Ronnie Aah! (*He drops the script on the table*) Catch me, Nurse! (*He does a mock swoon into a chair*)

Phoebe (*exasperated*) Ronnie, if you don't . . .

Ronnie (*his arms flapping*) I'm going! I'm going! Quick! In my coat pocket.

Doris (*as she feels in his coat pocket; not sure*) Ronnie, you're not *really* . . . (*She extracts an envelope from his pocket*) This what you . . . ?

Ronnie No, not that! That's my will; my solicitor'll want that! The other side.

Phoebe Ronnie Meadows, if you don't stop all this nonsense . . .

Doris (*to Ronnie, having produced a flat quarter bottle of brandy from the other pocket of his coat*) You mean—this? Brandy?

Ronnie (*after making a low gurgling noise, seizing the bottle and holding it to his lips for a time*) Aaah! Aah! That's better; just in time!

Doris (*laughing*) You idiot! You haven't unscrewed the top off. (*The laughing has made her head ache*) Ow! (*Her hand goes to her head, she staggers slightly*)

Phoebe (*to Doris; firmly*) You sit yourself down again, and don't move! (*To Ronnie*) And *you* . . .

Ronnie Yes, Matron?

Phoebe You get these things—(*picking up the first aid box and bowl and holding them out to Ronnie*)—out of here and down into the kitchen.

Ronnie (*after looking into the bowl, the water in which is somewhat bloody*) Aah!

Phoebe Now what?

Ronnie (*pointing gingerly into the bowl*) What's all this red . . . ? Dracula's supper? Please—it *is* tomato ketchup, isn't it?

Phoebe Taste it and see!

Ronnie (*again with a mock swoon*) Aaah!

Phoebe (*exasperated*) For heaven's sake . . . !

Smith, unnoticed by Phoebe, has entered R

I'll take these away. And, Ronnie, if you upset Doris with your fooling . . . (*She is moving R when she almost bumps into Smith. She stiffens*)

Ronnie and Doris are watching

Smith (*to Phoebe, very subserviently*) You finished with the first aid box?

Phoebe (*after the slightest pause; coldly*) I have.

Smith Then I'll take it, shall I? (*He holds out his hands towards the box*)

Phoebe puts the box down on a chair very deliberately

Phoebe (*deliberately turning away from Smith*) Doris—just sit quiet for a few minutes, and then I think you ought to go home.

Phoebe, ignoring Smith, marches off up R, with the bowl

Smith picks up the box, looks after Phoebe. Ronnie and Doris exchange questioning glances

Smith (*awkwardly, almost mumbling*) Lucky I 'appened to see this box in
the cupboard out there, wasn't it?
Ronnie (*quietly*) Yes. Thanks.
Smith Course—bein' new 'ere, I didn't know whether there was anything
in it or not; might've been empty for all I knew.
Ronnie H'm!
Smith But it *was* useful?
Ronnie Yes. Thanks. (*After an awkward pause*) Er—don't let us keep you
from getting on with your work.
Smith No. (*To Doris*) Feelin' better, miss?

Doris does not speak

'Orrible thing to 'appen. (*Slight pause*) Look! It's nothin' to do with me,
but . . .
Ronnie (*brightly*) How right you are!
Smith Eh?
Ronnie Obviously you're a man of brains!
Smith Eh?
Ronnie You're so right in everything you say.
Smith I don't . . . (*He is bewildered*)
Ronnie You said just now that it—whatever "it" is—has nothing to do
with you. You're right; it hasn't, so . . . (*He makes a "shoo-ing" gesture
with his hands*)
Smith (*after a glare at Ronnie*) Bloody funny, aren't you?

Smith exits L, muttering

*Ronnie moves up looking after him, making sure he has gone. Doris puts her
hands to her head, obviously in pain. Ronnie moves towards her*

Ronnie I say, you're not going to faint, are you? I'm no good with fainting
females!
Doris (*her hands still to her head*) Who is that fellow?
Ronnie New caretaker. Bit of a basket, if you ask me.
Doris (*still holding her head*) Phoebe doesn't seem to be over fond of him.
Ronnie No, she doesn't, does she? (*He looks R*)
Doris Well, God help him if he gets the wrong side of *her*. (*Suddenly*) Oh,
God! My head. Isn't half playing me up!

*Ronnie quickly unscrews the top from the brandy flask (it is a cup type of
top) and pours some brandy into it*

Ronnie (*at Doris's side, holding out the brandy*) Here. Drink some of this.
Doris (*after taking the brandy from him, about to drink*) You got this
specially for me, didn't you?
Ronnie (*sheepishly*) Huh-huh.
Doris (*after giving him a light kiss on the head, smiling*) And you know
very well Babycham's my tipple. (*She drinks some brandy*)
Ronnie (*eagerly*) If you'd rather have a . . .

Doris Are you kidding? (*She drinks again, emptying the top*)
Ronnie (*holding out the flask*) More?
Doris No.

Ronnie withdraws the flask

(*Smiling as she holds out the top*) Don't take me so literally.

Ronnie refills the top

You don't understand women, do you, Ronnie?
Ronnie (*with a grin*) I'd like to. How about it?
Doris How about what?
Ronnie (*still with a grin*) Us—getting married.
Doris (*laughing and ruffling his hair*) Idiot!
Ronnie But . . .
Doris You're an idiot, but a sweet one.
Ronnie (*still grinning*) You don't love me?
Doris (*slipping an arm around him affectionately*) I adore you. We all do.
You've a *way* with the ladies, haven't you?
Ronnie (*after the slightest pause*) A—a way? Yes, I suppose I have.

Doris smiles at him then takes a swig of brandy

Doris (*after the swig*) Ronnie . . .

Ronnie does not answer; just sits gazing into space

(*Noticing this*) Hey! I'm talking to *you*.
Ronnie (*with a little start*) Sorry. I was——
Doris —miles away.
Ronnie What were you going to say?
Doris (*after holding out the top to Ronnie*) When I first came in here—
tonight . . .
Ronnie (*pouring a little brandy into the top*) What an entrance! You *were*
in a state!
Doris (*impatiently*) I know. I know that, but—(*after taking a sip of brandy*)
—I—I—didn't actually *say* who I thought it was who'd . . . (*Anxiously*)
I didn't, did I?
Ronnie (*quietly*) Not in words—no.

They look at each other

But you've a very—"expressive" face—anyone ever told you that?—
and I don't think you left any of us in doubt as to—who it was you—
suspected. (*Slight pause*) But, Doris—honestly—you can't really think
it was—Philip? I mean—well, dammit, it's—it's too absurd.

*During Ronnie's speech, Margaret and Alan have appeared from up L.
They are moving forward, but on hearing Philip's name mentioned,
Margaret, with a gesture, stops Alan in his tracks, and with a hand on his
arm, draws him backwards. They disappear from view up L*

Doris (*meanwhile*) Is it?

Ronnie (*troubled*) Oh, God—if it was him! Poor Margaret! (*Slight pause*)
Doris—what makes you think . . . ? You're not—not certain, are you?

Doris (*after a slight pause; holding out the top*) I haven't finished the bottle,
have I?

Ronnie (*his thoughts elsewhere*) What? (*Realizing*) Oh, no, but—er—(*with
an attempt at lightness*)—this isn't Babycham, y'know.

Doris (*with a little giggle*) I get you! More expensive. (*Wagging a finger at
him*) Meany!

Ronnie (*pouring a little brandy into the top*) Here, I say! I'm not thinking
of the *expense*; it's the *strength* I'm worried about. You—you'll—
(*anxiously*)—be all right, won't you?

Doris (*after sipping the brandy*) D'you know the make of Philip's car—
and its number?

Ronnie What? No, I'm damned if I do. Cars don't interest me.

Doris (*hardly listening*) It's a Cortina, and the number's OCD three-nine-
four G.

Ronnie Well? What about it?

Doris You know the grubby little street that leads on to the bit of waste
land—just outside here?

Ronnie (*almost impatiently*) You mean Robert Street? It's due for demoli-
tion any time now; most of the houses are empty anyway. Why? What
about it?

Doris (*her voice just slightly slurred*) I passed Philip's car tonight, parked
half-way along it—that's what about it. (*She sips brandy*)

Ronnie (*after a pause*) What the devil would he be doing in his car down
there?

Doris You're missing the point, my love. He wasn't *in his car*.

Ronnie What?

Doris Philip's car, *yes*. Philip, *no*! (*She puts a hand in her coat pocket*)

Ronnie (*almost babbling*) But that doesn't mean—I mean—he might've
been . . .

Doris (*slightly more muzzy*) Listen, Angel-face—I don't want you to tell
me where he *might've* been, 'cos I'm telling you where he damn' well
was—and I'm not just talking out of the top of my hat which I'm not
wearing tonight. (*Slight pause. She lays a hand on Ronnie's shoulder*) I've
got proof, Honeybunch.

Ronnie Proof? What—er . . . ?

*Doris slowly withdraws her hand from her coat pocket. In it is a silk square
scarf of distinctive design*

(*With a start; almost loudly*) What the . . . ?

Doris Seen this before?

Ronnie (*blinking at the scarf, then at Doris*) Seen . . . ? No, I don't think
I . . . Oh, God, yes!

Doris 'Course you have. We presented it to Philip after his last production, didn't we?

Ronnie That's right; I remember. (*Taking the scarf from Doris and looking
at it*) Yes—yes, of course. (*Slight pause*) But what—where . . . ?

Doris When I came round—after I'd been attacked—I found I had that—
(*indicating the scarf*)—clutched in my hand. I must have grabbed at it
when—he came at me. (*She sips the brandy*) So you see why I hesitated
about getting the police here right away, don't you? You *see* that?
Ronnie (*mumbling*) Yes, of course.
Doris (*with another sip at the brandy*) But the point is—what does little
Doris do *now*? Any suggestions? (*She slurs the word "suggestions".
Realizing this*) Oo! 'Ark at me! (*Repeating the word with care*) "Su-ges-
tions." That's better, isn't it? (*She giggles*)
Ronnie (*hardly listening to her; looking at the scarf*) I can't believe . . .

Margaret, followed by Alan, comes on up L. *She moves near Ronnie. Alan
remains up* L

Margaret (*in surprise*) Oh, hello! I didn't know you were back already,
Ronnie. (*To Doris*) How are you now, darling? Feel well enough to
—to go home?

Ronnie, scarf in hands, is looking acutely embarrassed

Doris (*vaguely*) Home? But what about rehearsal?
Margaret Darling, you can't possibly rehearse, not after . . . Nobody
could expect you to, could they, Ronnie?
Ronnie (*babbling*) I—I . . .
Margaret (*suddenly, seeing the scarf in Ronnie's hand, in great surprise*) Oh!
Ronnie (*looking up*) What . . . ?
Margaret (*overlapping*) So *there* it is! And I searched . . . Ronnie, where
did you find it?
Ronnie (*blinking*) What . . . ?
Margaret (*taking the scarf from Ronnie's hands and opening it out as she
speaks*) Philip's scarf—the one we gave him after the last show he
produced.

Ronnie and Doris exchange furtive glances

When we got home after the last rehearsal—last Friday—he realized
he hadn't got it on—thought he must have left it here. I came down here
the next morning, but I couldn't find it anywhere, so we came to the
conclusion that, as it wasn't here, or in the car, it must have slipped off
in the street. We certainly thought we'd said good-bye to it.
Ronnie (*ingenuously*) You say Philip lost it—last week?
Margaret (*almost impatiently*) I've *just* told you. He . . .
Ronnie (*very happily*) Oh, well! That's fine! (*To her*) Isn't that fine, Doris?

Doris gives him a withering look

Margaret (*puzzled*) Look, I don't understand. What's the mystery? Doris
—this scarf? Has it something to do with—with your being attacked
tonight?
Doris (*not looking at Margaret*) Ronnie—there wouldn't—there *couldn't*
be just the tiniest drop more left in the bottle? (*She holds out the top*)
Could there?

Ronnie, avoiding looking at Margaret, pours a little brandy into the top

Ronnie (*half looking at Margaret, mumbling*) 'Scuse me! (*He takes a swig from the bottle himself*)

Margaret and Alan look at each other, then, Alan, after a glance at the scarf in Margaret's hand, moves away slightly

Margaret (*after following Alan with her eyes; to Ronnie and Doris*) If the orgy is over . . . !

Doris (*with mock disappointment*) Oh, is it over? (*Turning Ronnie's wrist so that the bottle is upside down, obviously empty. To Margaret, wryly*) It's over!

Margaret Good! Now! About this scarf—this scarf of Philip's . . .

Doris (*suddenly rising and moving away just a little shakily*) Forget it, darling.

Margaret What?

Doris I said forget it.

Margaret But I want to know how it—it got here.

Doris (*looking straight at Margaret*) Do you, Margaret? Are you sure of that? (*Slight pause*) I—I shall be in the "Ladies" if I'm wanted. (*She moves up stage with just the slightest trace of unsteadiness. As she is about to pass Alan she pats his cheek*) Darling boy! (*After passing him, turning*) Isn't he a darling boy, Margaret?

Margaret (*who has had her eyes on the scarf*) What—er—who . . . ? (*She turns to face Doris*)

Doris (*derisively*) "Who"? (*Looking towards the embarrassed Alan*) Why, Alan, of course! Who else? The Society isn't exactly *overrun* with darling boys—is it—(*looking at Margaret*)—darling? (*She smiles*) Well—as I said, if I'm wanted, Ronnie, I shall be in the ladies loo. (*She turns to go*)

Ronnie (*embarrassed, hardly realizing what he is saying*) It's all right. I'm coming along too.

Doris (*in mock horror*) Ronnie, per-*lease!*

Doris exits up R

Ronnie (*babbling, as he begins to follow her*) I didn't mean—I meant . . . (*To Margaret*) Excuse me! (*He almost stumbles off after Doris*)

Ronnie exits up R

There is an awkward pause. Alan is looking somewhat wretchedly at Margaret, who, with the scarf still in her hand, moves away, agitatedly

Margaret (*at last*) You see? She—Doris knows—or guesses.

Alan Knows what? You mean—about the scarf?

Margaret (*very sharply*) No, I don't. There's nothing *to* know about the scarf—except who found it, and where. (*Slight pause*) I mean about—us.

Alan Us?

Margaret (*impatiently*) Oh, for God's sake! You can't be as naïve as all that, Alan. I mean about our—our fooling about.

Alan (*hurt*) Margaret!

Margaret Well, what else can you call it? God! I must have been out of my mind. A married woman . . . (*Desperately*) Alan, I don't want to be hurtful, but you *must* see. I know I'm to blame; I—encouraged you, and I'm sorry, but—from now on—it's all over. I'm not going to have all the Society—laughing at me; and Philip—if he found out . . . Now do get that into your head. It's all over.

Alan It's no use talking like that. You can't turn your—your feelings off just like that—like a tap. You love me . . .

Margaret No!

Alan You love me. You've told me you do . . .

Margaret Oh, God!

Alan And I love you.

Margaret (*desperately*) Don't talk such damned nonsense. How old are you—twenty-one? And I'm what? Thirty-four, and a married woman. It's too absurd. Especially when I know damned well that if you didn't see me for a couple of months . . .

Alan I'd go out of my mind.

Margaret You'd forget all about me.

Alan No!

Margaret Alan—please. (*Moving away*) Haven't I got enough to worry about, without . . .

Alan You mean—Philip—and—that—scarf?

Margaret Why keep on about the scarf?

Alan What you said to Doris and Ronnie—about Philip losing it last week —that isn't true, is it?

Margaret (*turning on him*) Of course it's true.

Alan (*sharply*) You're lying!

Margaret Alan!

Alan (*almost shouting*) You're lying and you know it! You're trying to protect Philip . . .

Margaret (*urgently*) Keep your voice down!

Alan (*heedlessly, going on quickly*) You know—everybody knows; Doris made it plain enough to us all who it was'd attacked her.

Margaret (*almost shouting herself*) Shut up!

Smith, unnoticed by Margaret and Alan, enters quietly, and stands up L

Alan (*still loudly*) Philip—he's this—this "Prowler" fellow and you know it, don't you?

Margaret (*still fairly loudly*) No, I don't know it, and I won't believe it. (*Turning away*) I . . . (*She sees Smith. With almost a cry of horror*) Oh, God!

Alan (*going on*) He never lost that scarf last week. You never came here to find it. You . . .

Margaret (*topping him*) Alan!

Alan is silenced. He looks at Margaret, who, with her eyes, indicates Smith

Alan (*startled*) Oh! (*To Smith; completely flustered*) What—what do you . . . ? What are you . . . ?

Smith (*quietly, grinning*) Nothin' to do with me, of course, but I thought you might like to know you can be 'eard—er—*talking*—to each other nearly 'alf-way across the street. (*He moves down a little, then goes on*) Thought you might like to know that, 'cos—well—(*after looking at them both*)—you don't want everybody to know your private affairs, do you? (*He has taken a cigarette from behind his ear. To Margaret*) Got a light? Then we'll talk—*business*, shall we?

Margaret, with eyes on him, takes a lighter from her bag, or pocket, and holds it out to Smith. As she clicks it on, Alan suddenly dashes forward, snatches the lighter from Margaret's hand

Alan (*as he does this*) No!

Margaret (*surprised and alarmed*) Alan!

Alan (*turning to Smith; in a quiet but forceful voice*) You'll find your own lights, Mister. And in future you'll buy your own bloody smokes!

Smith (*after a moment; staggered*) What?

Alan Get off this stage, d'you hear? Get off, you blackmailing swine, or I'll . . . (*He approaches Smith threateningly*)

Margaret (*trying to stop him*) Alan, for God's sake!

Smith (*to Margaret, almost shouting*) Let him alone! Let's 'ear what he's going to do. But lay a hand on me, you young whippersnapper and I'll make things 'ot for you—*and* for 'er—(*pointing at Margaret*)—yes, *and* for that bastard of a husband of yours! 'E'd like to hear about what's goin' on between you two, wouldn't he? Give 'im something to think about *while he's in clink for attacking young girls*!

Alan (*shouting*) Shut your blasted . . . !

Smith (*topping him*) Christ! Call yourselves a Dramatic Society! More of a bloody Fornicating Society if you ask me.

Alan flies at Smith and grabs him by the throat

Alan Why you . . . !   ⎧ *speaking*
Margaret Alan—no! ⎨ *together*

Phoebe's voice is heard, near and loud, off R

Phoebe (*off*) Cut that out, Alan!

Alan, surprised on hearing Phoebe's voice, releases Smith

Phoebe appears R

(*Quietly*) Not a bad entrance that, was it? (*To Margaret*) Having trouble?

Margaret (*almost muttering*) Yes—a bit.

Phoebe (*very much in command*) Alan, get away from him.

Alan I'm going to . . . (*He half turns to Smith again*)

Phoebe No, you're not. You're going to do as you're told! *Come over here!*

Alan, after a moment's hesitation, moves away from Smith. Phoebe, after pausing and standing quite still for a moment with eyes on Smith, moves down to him

(*To Smith; quietly*) You trying to cause trouble?
Smith (*babbling*) I—I . . .
Phoebe I wouldn't—not if I were you.

Smith tries to give Phoebe a glare, fails, and after a slight pause goes off up R

Alan Good Lord, Phoebe! How did you manage that?
Phoebe (*cutting in*) Are we going to do any more rehearsing tonight or not? Where is everybody? (*To Margaret*) Where's that husband of yours?

There is a door slam off up L

Ah! Talk of the devil! I'd know that door slam anywhere.
Margaret (*to Phoebe, quickly and quietly*) Phoebe—please—don't *you* say anything to Philip about—well—about anything.
Phoebe (*with a broad grin*) You mean—I'm not to talk to him—not at all? Poor devil! On top of everything else he's going to have a dumb character actress on his hands. Oh well . . . !

Philip enters up L. He is worried, but rather quiet, for him

Philip (*seeing Phoebe and the others*) Ah! (*To Phoebe*) Any of the others here?

Phoebe gesticulates, pointing off R

And how's Doris? Is she all right now?

Phoebe nods her head once or twice

Can she rehearse tonight, or . . . ?

Phoebe gives an "I don't know" shrug of the shoulders

(*Grinning*) And what the hell's the matter with *you*? Lost your voice?

Phoebe nods her head vigorously

My God! I've experienced some tough rehearsals in my time, but tonight's is certainly one to remember! Well, we'd better get the others up, and . . . (*He begins to move up R*)

Phoebe puts a hand on his shoulder, stopping him. She then indicates in dumb show that she will go and get the others

(*With just a little irritation*) Oh, for God's sake, Phoebe . . .

Phoebe clicks her fingers, looking at Alan. She gestures to him that he is to come with her. She does this very authoritatively

Phoebe, have you been drinking—heavily?

Phoebe nods her head more vigorously, then again gestures to Alan that he is to come with her. She begins to move up R

(*To Alan*) You'd better go with her. We don't want her falling down those damned stairs. (*Moving to his table*) She's obviously completely sloshed! (*He has his back to Phoebe*)

Phoebe turns as if to protest vigorously, thinks better of it, and stamps off up R.
Alan follows her off

There is a slight pause, then Margaret and Philip look at each other almost warily

(*At last, with a nod of the head up* R) Phoebe—what is she playing at? She isn't tight, of course.
Margaret Of course not.
Philip Then what . . . ?
Margaret She was only—fooling.
Philip Fooling? You mean—trying to introduce a little light relief into the—melodramatic atmosphere that seems to have found its way into this rehearsal?

Margaret is silent

(*After a slight pause; awkwardly*) Look—this is the first chance I've had to speak to you since—since Doris—practically accused me—*me*, if you please—of attacking her tonight.
Margaret (*quietly*) Well?
Philip (*after a sharp look at her*) "Well?" For God's sake, is that all you've got to say—"Well"? (*Another pause*) Margaret, you—you don't believe that I did attack her, do you?
Margaret (*quietly*) *Someone* did.
Philip (*with a burst*) Dammit! I know that. But why should you think . . .
Margaret What I think doesn't matter much, I suppose. The point is—Doris thinks so.
Philip But *why* me, for God's sake? Why?

Margaret has had the scarf concealed behind her back. She now holds it out for Philip to see. Philip, still at his table, looks at the scarf for a moment, then goes to Margaret and takes the scarf from her

(*In genuine surprise*) This is mine; the scarf I lost last week.

(*He looks at Margaret. She returns his look*

(*In another burst*) Look! For the love of God, let's cut out all the scene building, the dramatic pauses and what not. What's all this about? Where did this scarf come from?
Margaret (*steadily*) Why should it have "come from" anywhere?

Philip (*bewildered*) What?

Margaret You lost it *here*, last week, didn't you?

Philip You know damn' well I did. (*He goes to his table and automatically puts the scarf down on it*)

Margaret I know you *told* me you did.

Philip (*after beating his clenched fist on the table*) And why should I tell you I *did* if I *didn't*? I haven't seen that scarf since last Friday night.

Margaret looks at him sceptically

I haven't. I haven't I tell you.

Margaret (*still with her eyes on him*) Philip—do you swear to that?

Philip (*after controlling himself*) Since that seems necessary to make you even begin to believe me—yes, I do. (*Slight pause*) *Do* you believe me?

Margaret (*rather flatly*) Yes, of course.

Philip (*with a little sarcasm*) You *could* have put a little more sincerity into that line; nevertheless—thank you. (*Slight pause*) And now—perhaps you'll tell me—why all this hoo-ha about the scarf, anyway?

Margaret (*after a slight pause*) Whoever attacked Doris tonight was wearing it.

Philip (*gaping at her*) What?

Margaret Doris says she must have grabbed it in the struggle. And, of course, she recognized it.

Philip Oh—my—God! That's why she thinks it was me!

Margaret shrugs her shoulders

And she's told you that—to your face?

Margaret No—she hasn't.

Philip Then . . . ?

Margaret I—I overheard her telling Ronnie.

Philip That she thought it was me—because of the scarf?

Margaret You can't blame her for thinking it.

Philip Who else has she told it to, for God's sake?

Margaret I don't *think* she's told Phoebe, but . . .

Philip (*after a slight pause*) But what? Let's have it.

Margaret (*quietly*) Alan knows. (*Slight pause*) He—he happened to be with me when I overheard Doris telling Ronnie.

Philip (*controlling himself with difficulty*) In other words, half the blasted Society knows and the other half soon will!

Margaret *Does* that matter? You say you didn't do it. Then you've only got to say where you were at the time of the attack, haven't you?

Philip (*somewhat shaken*) Yes. Yes—of course.

Margaret looks at him, expecting him to say where he was. When he does not do so, she turns away a little. Philip is watching her

Margaret (*after a definite pause*) Then there's—something else.

Philip (*witheringly*) There couldn't be!

Margaret (*turning to him*) That caretaker—Smith; he seems to know about it.

Philip That—bastard! What makes you think he . . . ?
Margaret He's hinted as much.
Philip Hinted? Who to? To you?
Margaret Well—in a way—yes.
Philip (*beginning to seeth*) "In a way"? What the hell do you mean "in a way"? And what the devil were you doing, chatting to a louse like that?
Margaret (*also beginning to flare up a little*) I wasn't *chatting* to him!
Philip Well, dammit, he couldn't have told you in dumbshow!

Margaret is about to shout at Philip, but controls herself

Margaret (*quietly but nervously, choosing her words*) Before you came in just now—he and Alan had a—a flare-up.
Philip (*almost with a laugh*) Good God! Even little Alan, eh? What about?
Margaret (*desperately*) What does it matter what about? That man just gets everyone's goat. (*Slight pause*) He said something—offensive to Alan, and—started abusing the Society—and you.
Philip What did he say about me?
Margaret (*hesitantly*) He—he . . .
Philip Well?
Margaret (*almost wildly, evasively*) I can't remember *just* what he said, but it was something about you—attacking young girls.
Philip (*after looking at Margaret for a moment, puzzled*) Where is he now, d'you know? Is he still in the building?
Margaret I don't know. Why?
Philip I want to see him. I want to see him badly. If he's thinking of going to the police with that tale, I want to make sure he's in bloody agony every step of the way. (*He moves to go off* L)
Margaret (*quickly*) No, Philip, don't. Leave him alone.
Philip (*incredulously*) *Leave him . . . ?*
Margaret I don't think there's the slightest likelihood of his going to the police. Blackmail's more in his line.

Margaret moves away, her back to Philip

Philip What makes you think . . . ?

Phoebe's voice is heard in the distance off R

Phoebe (*off*) Listen! How many more times am I to tell you all—you're wanted on stage.
Margaret (*quickly*) What are you going to say to them all? Perhaps they know about the scarf by now. What are you going to say?

Voices are heard in the distance off R

Philip (*moving to his table*) Say? Nothing.

The voices draw nearer

Margaret You mean—you're going on rehearsing—as if nothing had happened?

Philip As far as I'm concerned, nothing *has* happened. And just to show 'em it hasn't . . . (*He picks up the scarf from the table and ties it loosely round his neck*)

Margaret (*seeing this*) Philip! You can't . . . !

Philip sits in the chair by his table and almost strikes a pose. The ends of the scarf are outside his jacket

Philip (*calling out*) Everybody on stage!

Margaret (*desperately*) Philip . . . !

Phoebe rushes on up R

Phoebe (*as she comes on*) They're coming! They're coming! And I warn you, they're practically in a state of revolt! It looks as if there'll be no coffee tonight, and . . . (*Casually, as she notices Philip is wearing the scarf*) What's the matter? You starting a cold? (*She immediately crosses to Margaret*) Boiled onions, darling; they're the best thing for a cold. Give him them in bed. *And* see that he keeps his bowels open. (*Her voice lowers as she goes on talking, inaudibly, to Margaret*)

Alan and Pat enter up R

Alan (*as he enters*) Ronnie's a heck of a time finding him! Why the devil does he have to mess about with the damn' thing tonight? He could have left it until tomorrow.

Philip What "damn' thing", and who's messing about with it?

Alan (*turning to Philip*) That fellow Smith. He's . . . (*He stops speaking as he notices the scarf. His eyes register blank incredulity*) Oh! (*He stands gaping at Philip*)

Philip (*after a slight pause, quietly*) "Oh" what?

Alan (*uncomfortably*) Er—er—(*lamely*)—nothing.

Philip (*quietly*) What has Smith done?

Alan (*as if he had not heard*) What?

Philip does not speak

(*Pulling himself together*) Oh—he—he's started to disconnect the boiler in the kitchen, and just gone off and left it. We know it wants seeing to, but it did work. Now we can't make any coffee. I wouldn't mind betting he's done it deliberately. Ronnie's gone across to the pub to find him.

Philip Can't *you*—connect it up again?

Alan Me?

Philip Well, you're an electrician, aren't you? That's your job.

Alan Yes, but . . .

Philip Or would it be against union rules?

Alan I could get it working again in five minutes, but I don't want to have a row with Smith. I might murder him.

Philip (*smoothly*) Well, why not *do* that—*and* mend the boiler?

Doris, still with the bandage round her head, enters up R. *Her speech is occasionally ever so slightly slurred, and sometimes she is a little uncertain on her feet*

Doris (*as she enters*) Hya! (*She is quite bright*) This is a devil, isn't it? The boiler in the kitchen . . .
Philip (*cutting in coldly*) We've heard about the boiler—in detail.
Doris (*turning to face Philip*) But we can't have any coffee and . . . (*Her voice trails away. She stands quite still, staring at the scarf round Philip's neck*)

There is a dead pause

Philip (*fingering the ends of his scarf nonchalantly; quietly*) Are you feeling better now? (*Slight pause*) Do you want to rehearse tonight or—or what?

Doris stands staring at the scarf, then at Philip for a moment. Then she begins to giggle quietly

(*Coldly*) Apparently—"we are amused"!
Doris (*still giggling*) Margaret—you were quite right.
Margaret What?
Doris (*turning to Philip again*) Margaret and I went together to buy your scarf. She *said* that one—(*indicating the scarf*)—would suit you. I didn't think it would, but—she was right; it does. It suits you admirably.
Philip (*coldly*) You've seen me wearing it before.
Doris Yes, darling, but—not to such good effect.
Philip (*after a slight pause*) Would you mind answering my question?
Doris Question . . . ?
Philip Do you feel up to rehearsing, or not? (*Indicating*) Your head —is it . . . ?
Doris (*gaily*) Of *course* I'm going to rehearse! I'm a trouper—didn't you know that? A trouper—like Phoebe! (*She goes to Phoebe and puts an arm round her*) Dear Phoebe! (*Declaiming*) "Sixty years behind a flat, and never missed a cue!"
Phoebe (*almost growling*) I'd have appreciated the compliment more if you'd taken at least three years off!

Ronnie enters up R

Alan (*to Ronnie, quickly*) You found Smith, Ronnie?
Ronnie (*vaguely*) Eh? (*Pulling himself together*) Oh, yes, he's over at the pub. Says he'll come and fix the boiler when . . .
Doris When what—when we've all gone home?
Ronnie When he feels like it—that's what he said.
Doris Charming!
Ronnie (*moving to Doris's side as he speaks*) Are you feeling—er—all right?
Doris Fine, darling, fine!
Ronnie (*muttering*) Wish I was! I'd sell my soul for a coffee.

Doris (*taking Ronnie by the arm*) Ronnie—look!

Ronnie What? Where?

Doris propels him round to face Philip

(*As he is being turned*) What . . . ? (*As he sees the scarf; under his breath*) God!

Ronnie gapes at Philip for a moment. Philip sits returning Ronnie's look steadily

(*At last, acutely embarrassed*) Er—er—are we going to *begin* again? Rehearsing, I mean.

Philip If you feel so disposed.

Ronnie Eh? (*Babbling*) Oh, yes—yes. I'm disposed.

Philip Thank you.

Ronnie Don't mention it. (*Almost tottering to his table*) Stand by, everybody! Clear stage!

Philip (*rising, and acting heavily*) But . . . before we *do* begin . . . !

Everyone turns to him. Philip, thoroughly enjoying giving a performance, walks slowly and silently C *and stands down by the floats with his back to the audience*

(*After a slight pause*) Before—we do begin—I should like to know if we can expect—*another* interruption—tonight.

The others look at him, puzzled

Margaret (*after a slight pause*) Philip, what do you . . . ?

Philip, rather grandly, waves her to silence

Philip (*speaking generally*) I cannot believe that your, apparent, craving for coffee has driven from your minds all thought of the incident which occurred earlier this evening. (*With a little laugh*) No, no! I'm sure it hasn't. I'm certain you have already dealt with it;—er—*got the necessary wheels turning.*

Doris (*muttering to Phoebe*) That's a line from some play or other.

Ronnie I wish you'd tell us what the devil you're talking about.

Philip (*still "acting"*) With pleasure! (*Quickly*) I apologize! "Pleasure" is hardly the—apt word—as I happen to be talking about—the attack on Doris.

The others give a start

Has anything been done about it? *Ronnie?*

Ronnie (*almost jumping out of his seat*) Eh?

Philip Have the authorities been informed; and are we to expect hordes of policemen arriving here at any moment? (*He pauses, then barks almost accusingly at Ronnie*) Well—are we?

Ronnie (*babbling*) I—*I* haven't sent for . . .

Philip (*topping him*) And why not? (*With pained patience*) Dammit, man, you *are* the stage manager!

Ronnie (*in a pathetic burst*) My job is to see the curtain goes up and down, and see the artists are on stage when they should be, and check that all the "props" are there and—every damn' thing else, but I didn't know I was supposed to . . . (*He buries his face in his hands*)

Doris (*rushing over to Ronnie and putting an arm around him protectingly*) There, there, my poppet! Don't you let our big, hulking, nasty producer upset you!

Philip *What?*

He moves a step towards Doris, who immediately turns facing him, and gives a "bull-doggish" growl—baring her teeth

Doris Grrrrrrrrrhh!

Philip, unconsciously jumps back a pace

Philip (*fuming*) Now look . . . !

Doris You sadistic bully!

Philip *What?*

Doris You—you attacker of—(*slight pause*)—of defenceless stage managers!

Philip (*with an almost despairing howl*) For God's sake . . . !

Doris (*after kissing Ronnie's head lightly, coming over to Philip*) Listen! What happened tonight—happened to *me*. Agreed?

Philip (*almost shouting*) Of course it did. We *know* that!

Doris (*with placating gesture*) O.K.! O.K.! We're agreed on one thing at any rate! It happened to me, and it's for me to say if I want the police brought into it or not. Agreed?

Philip But damn it all . . . !

Doris (*overlapping*) Do you agree, or don't you?

Philip *Yes*, but . . .

Doris O.K.! O.K.! (*Turning to the others*) You heard, everybody? (*With a wave of her hand towards Philip*) God Almighty's understudy has agreed with me—*twice!* (*In a quieter voice*) Well, I don't *want* the police brought in. That is *my* decision. *MINE*. See?

Philip (*looking hard at her*) I—I *presume* you have a reason?

Doris I have.

Philip What?

Doris (*firmly, looking straight at him*) And *that's* mine, too. D'you mind?

Philip, after looking at Doris for a moment, moves to his table

Philip (*suddenly, curtly*) Rehearsal dismissed for five minutes!

General exclamations of surprise from everyone except Ronnie,. who is still sitting at his table, elbows on it and head in hands

Clear stage, everybody. Go and get yourselves lost—all of you . . .

Doris the first to begin to go off

Except Doris!

Doris (*stopping in her tracks*) Oi! Oi! (*Grinning*) The Maiden's Prayer is about to be answered! (*She moves back again*)

Margaret (*to Phoebe, as they move slowly* R) Do you realize you and I haven't uttered one word of this play so far tonight?

Phoebe I do. But you're not complaining about *that*, are you?

Alan (*speaking generally*) Let's go up to one of the dressing-rooms, shall we?

Phoebe We've *been* up to one of the dressing-rooms a dozen times tonight.

Pat exits R

Alan (*brightly*) Yes, I know, but . . . Anyone got a pack of cards? I'll show you some tricks!

Phoebe (*throwing up her hands*) God in heaven!

Phoebe exits R

Margaret (*as she and Alan begin to move*) Much more sensible if *you* were to get that boiler working.

Margaret and Alan exit R

Doris (*moving to Ronnie and nudging him*) Oi! Rip Van Winkle!

Ronnie (*lifting his head from his hands; dazedly*) Eh? What?

Doris Scram!

Ronnie (*blankly*) Eh?

Doris Beat it!

Ronnie (*still bemused*) What? (*Rising*) Why?

Doris I'm going to be seduced.

Ronnie looks at her blankly

Yes! (*With a jerk of the head towards Philip*) I appear to have found favour in the eyes of the Great One. I can't let a chance like that slip, can I?

Ronnie (*vaguely, as he begins to move* R) Oh—well—good luck.

As Ronnie is about to go, Doris suddenly moves to him

Doris Ronnie . . . !

Ronnie (*stopping, still somewhat vague*) Yes?

Doris (*almost anxiously*) You're—all right, aren't you?

Ronnie All right?

Doris (*slightly puzzled*) You don't seem to be quite—"with it".

Ronnie (*grinning faintly*) With what? Your seduction? I don't *intend* to be!

Ronnie exits up R

Doris stands looking after him for a moment, then turns and comes down

Doris (*after looking at Philip for a split second, with a half smile*) Well—do
I strip *myself*, or do you . . . ?

Philip (*irritably*) Stop talking gibberish! (*He looks at her for a moment;
with a little laugh*) God! You're a tough nut, aren't you?

Doris Come again?

Philip I suppose you really *were* attacked this evening?

Doris (*after a slight pause*) You know damn' well I was.

Philip I can only congratulate you on your remarkable recovery.

Doris But *not*, I imagine, on my—lucky escape.

Philip (*after a slight pause, quietly*) It *wasn't me*, y'know.

Doris looks at him, but is silent

I can explain—about this scarf.

Doris You needn't. Margaret has already—"explained".

Philip But . . . ?

Doris She hasn't "explained" about your car.

Philip *What* about it?

Doris It was parked not three minutes' walk away from where—it happened—and you weren't in it. (*Quickly*) And it *was* your car; no use
saying it wasn't.

Philip (*after a slight pause*) I can explain about the car—that is, if you
insist?

Doris is silent

(*After another pause*) You and Margaret—you're good friends, aren't
you?

Doris You know we are.

Philip I imagine she's told you—something of our—domestic life?

Doris nods

(*With some bitterness*) Has she told you that about three years ago there
was—another man?

Doris (*genuinely surprised*) No!

Philip That we almost parted?

Doris, staggered, shakes her head

Or that now—there's someone else?

Doris Do you know that—for sure?

Philip No. Not for sure, but—(*sardonically*)—the signs—they're all there.

Doris The—signs?

Philip waves a dismissing hand

Do you know—*who* it is?

Philip No, but—and now we come to the explanation about the car.
(*Slight pause*) This afternoon I—I tried to catch her out.

Doris (*under her breath, with distaste*) Oh, God!

Philip (*aware of her tone*) I know! I know! But wait until you're married,
my girl! (*Slight pause*) I rang her at lunch time to say I'd be kept at the

office and wouldn't see her until rehearsal tonight—that I'd come straight here.

Doris Well?

Philip When I rang I was speaking from a phone-box not a hundred yards from our house.

Doris But your works are three miles out of town.

Philip After lunch—a quick one in the canteen—I drove back here and —*and listen to this*—parked the car in Robert Street, where you saw it this evening. If you'd troubled to feel the radiator you'd've found it stone cold. It had been there since half past one in the afternoon. I didn't want Margaret seeing the car in the town, and I knew she was hardly likely to be around there—Robert Street.

Doris And—and you're telling me you spent the afternoon—spying on your wife?

Philip I'm telling you that's what I *intended* to do, but—(*he shrugs his shoulders*)—she never left the house until she came to rehearsal this evening, and—nobody went into it. But that doesn't prove anything. It doesn't mean that . . .

Doris (*suddenly, quickly and quietly*) Philip!

Philip (*almost startled*) What . . . ?

Doris, with head and eyes, indicates just over the footlights where Smith is crossing from L *to* R *towards the steps to the stage*

(*Under his breath*) Christ!

Smith mounts the steps and moves up R

Philip and Doris watch him

Smith (*suddenly turning and addressing Philip, with an insolent grin*) I understand you've been complainin' 'cos' the boiler in the kitchen isn't workin'. I'd better see about it, 'adn't I?

Smith exits R

There is a slight pause

Philip (*almost with venom*) Damn and blast that fellow! (*He moves up* R *and looks off for a moment*) How the devil did a rat like that ever get his job? (*He returns down stage*)

Doris Never mind about *him*. What . . . ?

Philip (*overlapping*) I wonder how much he heard? I wouldn't mind betting he was out there—(*indicating the auditorium*)—at the back, listening to every bloody word!

Doris Does it matter one hoot if he was?

Philip Yes, it does! He knows already that you—suspect me.

Doris (*in utter surprise*) What? What are you talking about? How could he? I don't know the fellow; I've never spoken to him in my life. Philip, you don't think that *I* . . . ?

Philip (*irritably*) Of course I don't! But he has hinted to Margaret.
Doris (*dazed*) He has? Hinted what for heaven's sake?
Philip Just that; that you think it was me who attacked you.
Doris (*bewildered*) I don't get this. I'm sorry, but I just don't get it.
   (*Pointing* R) He—that fellow has . . . ?
Philip (*almost muttering*) Margaret said something about—about . . .
Doris (*more bewildered*) Look! I've taken a crack on the head, and I've
   had too much brandy tonight; I *know* that, but right now I'm neither
   unconscious nor blind drunk; at least, I didn't *think* I was! But when you
   start talking about Smith and me . . . (*Desperately*) For God's sake.
Philip (*loudly*) If Smith tries it on! But *let* him! By God! Let him just try!
Doris (*to herself*) Doris, old girl, you're going up the pole! There's not a
   thing wrong with you, except—you're going *up the pole*!
Philip I've never, ever wanted to commit murder before, but . . .

Suddenly there is a loud scream of terror from Pat in the distance off R

   What the hell . . . ?
Doris Completely up the pole!

*Quick footsteps are heard approaching, also several voices calling question-
ingly, followed by more—and several—footsteps running down a staircase*

Philip What is it? (*Moving up* R) What's happened?

   Pat, in a state bordering on hysteria, runs on R. *She passes Philip, stands
   looks round wildly, then runs to Doris, who immediately puts her arms
   around her*

Doris Pat . . . ?
Philip (*coming down stage*) Pat . . . what . . . ?
Pat (*sobbing*) That man—the caretaker . . . !
Philip (*loudly*) Smith? What's he done now?
Pat He—he's lying on the floor in the kitchen. I think—I'm *sure*—he's
   dead!

   The CURTAIN *falls quickly*

ACT III

The same; 7.45 p.m., a fortnight later

The scene is set as at the end of Act II, except that Philip's table and chair, and Ronnie's table and chair have been removed

When the CURTAIN *rises the stage is empty. After a moment Pat enters quickly down* L. *She is obviously in an emotional state. After moving* C *she looks off in the direction she came from, then, sobbing into a handkerchief, sits on one of the three chairs representing a settee. After a slight pause Alan enters down* L

Alan (*as he enters*) Damn them! Damn the lot of them!

In this opening scene, Alan speaks his lines somewhat flatly. Pat, on the other hand, overplays hers

Nothing but pointless questions! "Where were you when the body was found?" "But if you were *there* at such and such a time . . ." God! It makes you sick! (*He comes down near Pat. Impatiently*) And why are you sitting here all by yourself, moping? Why don't you join in the—the fun?

Pat (*somewhat wildly*) Fun? You call it fun?

Alan The police seem to be enjoying it, anyway.

Pat I can't stand it! All this—mystery—suspicion everywhere!

Alan No need for *you* to worry yourself. There's no suspicion as far as you're concerned. (*With a bitter laugh*) You're the one person who . . .

Pat (*sharply*) Who what?

Alan Don't jump down my throat like that! I was merely going to say you are the only one of us who is completely in the clear.

Pat (*rising and moving around distractedly*) They'll question me though, won't they! They'll probe and probe!

Alan For heaven's sake sit down and keep calm.

Pat Calm? How can I keep calm when . . . ?

Alan Sit down!

Pat (*loudly*) No!

Alan Sit down! (*He takes her by the arm and almost forces her to sit on the settee*) Y'know, it's quite ridiculous, the way you're taking all this. It has nothing whatsoever to do with you. (*He moves behind the settee*)

Pat It has! It has!

Alan (*putting his hands on Pat's shoulders*) Now listen, my dear . . .

Pat (*instantly leaping to her feet and moving quickly away. Shouting*) Don't do that!

Alan What's the *matter* with you?

Pat I don't like being—mauled; not when . . .

Alan Mauled! Thanks very much!

Pat (*wildly*) Why don't you go away—leave me alone?

Alan I'll tell you what I'm *going* to do! (*Grabbing her by the arms and shaking her, somewhat half-heartedly*) I'm going to stop you behaving like a hysterical little fool!

Pat (*screaming*) Let go of me! Let go of me!

Alan Not till you've got it into your head that this has nothing to do with you.

Pat (*wildly*) Don't keep saying that! It has everything to do with me! You don't understand. (*Struggling, shouting*) Let me go! Let me go!

Alan Damn you! Do you want to bring all the others in here?

Pat (*hysterically*) Bring them! I don't care. They'll have to know sooner or later! (*She begins to scream*) Let me go! Let me go! (*She struggles*)

Alan suddenly gives her a sharp slap across the face. Pat immediately stops screaming, but continues sobbing

Alan Perhaps *that* will quieten you down!

Pat (*after collapsing into the "settee"*) Get the police. Ask them to come in here. I want to tell them the truth. I can't keep it to myself any longer.

Alan Keep what? What are you talking about for God's sake? You can't tell the police anything.

Pat (*with a wild, unnatural laugh*) That's where you're wrong! I can tell them something they'll be very glad to know!

Alan What are you . . .

Pat I can tell them that—he—was—*my father*!

Alan *What?*

Phoebe enters up R

At exactly the same moment Philip's voice is heard from the back of the auditorium

Philip (*calling*) Hold it! *Hold it!*

Alan and Pat immediately stop "acting" and look out front. Phoebe stops in her tracks

Philip begins to come from the back of the hall to the steps leading on to the stage

(*As he comes down*) Sorry, Phoebe, but I'm going to take that scene again. I can't leave it as it is.

Phoebe turns her eyes heavenward, then goes off R

Philip is not so bombastic as in previous scenes

(*As he mounts the steps on to the stage*) Now, listen, you kids! You're grand on your *lines*; you've got *them* all right, but the way you're playing them at the moment . . . ! There's no—no *balance* to the scene. Alan, you're as flat as a burst tyre.

Alan (*sulkily*) Sorry!

Philip And, Pat, darling, you're just screaming your head off like a Billingsgate fishwife.

Pat (*near to tears*) I'm sorry.

Philip (*realizing Pat is upset; puzzled, and gently*) Now then! Now then! Now then! No need to upset yourself about it. Nothing we can't put right by talking it over. (*With a wave of the hand*) Sit down, both of you.

Pat is about to sit on the "settee" but, realizing Alan is moving to sit beside her, she moves, unobtrusively, to a chair and sits on it. Alan notices Pat's move away and looks towards her puzzled. Philip has also noticed the move and is also puzzled. Alan sits on the "settee"

Now then! (*He rubs his hands "businesslike"*) Your entrance, Pat; that was fine. Just the right speed, and the tension was there. The move to the settee—that was O.K. It was after Alan came on you seemed to go—I dunno quite, but . . . (*Realizing Pat is still upset, he turns to Alan*) And, Alan! That entrance of yours! I'm sorry, old lad, but it was way down on the floor. You're supposed to be absolutely *fuming* when you come on. You've been through a hell of a time with the police. They've been hammering questions at you for over half an hour—you mention that later on—and you've just left them and come straight in here. Your entrance should be an absolute *burst*. (*He acts the lines*) "Damn them! Damn the lot of them! Nothing but pointless questions", et cetera, et cetera. See what I mean?

Alan nods unenthusiastically

(*Turning to Pat again*) And, Pat—when Alan puts his hands on you from behind the settee—I know you're supposed to "freeze"—to stiffen —then move away, but, darling, the way you did it—it was much too exaggerated—as if you thought—well, as if you thought Alan was going to kill you.

Pat, who has been looking down on the floor, looks up with a start—then looks towards Alan. Alan has also given a start, and looks embarrassed. Philip, realizing he has said the wrong thing, is temporarily silenced. There is a very definite and awkward pause before he goes on

(*At last, still to Pat*) And all your outbursts, darling—far, far too wild.

Pat (*her eyes leaving Alan; almost vaguely*) I thought I was *supposed* to be hysterical in this scene.

Philip Of *course* you are! But *acting* hysteria is very different from actually being hysterical—and that's what I felt you were just now. However *wildly* the character is supposed to behave, the person *playing* it must *always* be in complete control of his or her voice and emotions, otherwise to those "out front" the performance comes over as just an

incoherent and embarrassing screaming session. Remember that, Pat—
to Alan)—and you, too, Alan! *Always*—complete control of your voice
—your emotions—and your body! (*He sees that Pat is obviously troubled.*
Smiling) Do I sound like—"Miss Fanthorpe's Academy of Dramatic
Art"?

Phoebe's head comes round a curtain up R

Phoebe's head disappears round the curtain

Philip (*after smiling in the direction of Phoebe*) Now come on! Let's run
the scene again, shall we?

Alan exits down L

Pat is still seated in the chair

(*With just a little irritation*) Pat! Come along! The scene again, darling.

Pat shakes her head

(*Surprised*) What? What's the matter?
Pat (*after a pause, looking down; quietly*) I don't want to go on with it.
Philip (*puzzled*) You mean you don't want to rehearse the scene again?
Pat I don't want to go on with the play—at all.
Philip (*after a pause*) Not . . . Are you serious?
Pat (*quietly*) Yes.

Alan comes just into view down L.
After a second, Phoebe just appears up R

Philip (*coldly*) You want to—throw the part in; that's what you mean?

Again Pat nods

You realize we've only a fortnight to production date?

Pat is silent

And that we haven't another suitable juvenile girl in the company—and
God knows where we'd get one at this stage?

*Pat is still silent. After looking at her for quite a while. Philip turns and looks
down* L

(*Calling quietly*) Ronnie? You in the prompt corner?
Pat (*wretchedly*) Please—don't bring . . .

Ronnie, open script in hand, pops on from down L

Ronnie (*quite brightly*) Yes?
Philip (*to Pat; coldly*) What were you going to say?
Pat (*almost in a whisper*) Please don't bring everyone here.

Philip Why not? They've all got to be told, haven't they? (*To the others*) I presume you all heard? Pat wants to throw up her part—a fortnight before we open. (*With some bitterness*) Charming, isn't it?

Phoebe (*to Philip; not nastily*) Now, now! You've been almost lovable tonight—so far. Don't go back to form! (*She crosses to Pat, slipping an arm round her*) Pat, darling . . .

Pat (*quietly*) Phoebe, I just don't want to go on—that's all there is to it.

Phoebe (*gently*) No, it isn't. Why don't you say what it really is?

Pat again looks round, at Ronnie, then longer at Alan

Alan (*at last; to Pat, uncomfortably*) Why are you looking at *me* like that? I—I haven't—done anything, have I?

Pat (*desperately*) I can't . . . (*Moving to Philip*) Can I talk to you—alone?

Philip Yes, of course, but—this is a company problem, and as Phoebe is the secretary of the Society I think she should be here as well.

Pat (*involuntarily, and with some alarm*) Oh, but . . .

Phoebe (*with just a tinge of sharpness*) But what?

Pat is silent. Phoebe does not take her eyes off her

(*At last, quietly*) Well, do I stay or don't I?

Pat (*after a moment's hesitation*) Yes. Yes, of course, Phoebe. I'd be—grateful. (*She sits on the "settee"*)

Ronnie (*brightly*) Surely you want Uncle Ronnie here? He could give you of his wisdom.

Phoebe He could *not*. He hasn't any to spare.

Alan moves near Pat

Alan (*awkwardly, but very gently*) Pat—this—your giving up the part—it hasn't anything to do with me—*has* it?

Pat looks up at him for a moment. Alan, almost unconsciously takes her hand in his. Phoebe, noticing this, gives a wolf whistle

(*Very embarrassed*) Oh, shut up, Phoebe! (*He drops Pat's hand quickly, but speaks to her*) It *hasn't*, has it, Pat?

Phoebe Young man!

Alan What?

Phoebe (*wagging a finger at him*) 'Oppit!

Alan But . . .

Phoebe (*sharply*) Pronto!

Alan moves away. Ronnie joins him

Ronnie (*to Alan*) Do you know—something's *occurred* to me!

Alan What?

Ronnie We're neither of us *wanted* here.

Alan In that case—what are we waiting for? (*He moves up* R)

Philip (*fairly sharply*) Don't go far away. Stay in the hall.

And tell Doris and Margaret to stand by as well. We may want you all in a few minutes, unless—we can persuade Pat to ... (*He looks towards Pat for a moment*) Right! (*Waving a dismissing hand at Alan and Ronnie*) Off!

Alan and Ronnie exit up R

Philip moves up and calls after them

And we don't want any ears flapping in the wings! (*Coming down*) Well —*now*! What's all this about?

Phoebe (*wagging a finger at him*) Now none of that "wide-eyed Winnie" stuff! You know very well what it's all about. It's about the bogey that's been hanging over the whole lot of us for the last fortnight—if only we'd admit it.

Philip (*after heaving a very troubled sigh*) Smith! Oh, God!

Pat covers her face with her hands

Phoebe (*nodding, as her arm tightens around Pat*) Yes—Smith.

Philip (*in a little burst*) Can't we forget about him?

Phoebe I don't think any of us are shedding any tears over him.

Pat (*almost wildly*) But he was killed, Phoebe; he was killed.

Philip (*quietly, firmly*) And we've been told *how* he was killed, haven't we?

Pat and Phoebe are silent

(*Impatiently*) You were at the inquest, Pat. Dammit, you had to give evidence of finding him.

Phoebe (*with brightness*) And you did it perfectly—sensibly. Every word as clear as a bell. I was right at the back and I didn't miss a syllable! It was all I could do to stop giving you a round of applause on your exit. (*To Philip*) *You* weren't so hot, by the way; you got yourself into a bit of a tizz-woz.

Philip Phoebe—please!

Phoebe Sorry!

Philip I know you mean well, but ... (*To Pat*) Pat, darling, what's worrying you about—about Smith? You heard the Coroner's verdict. *He* was quite satisfied it was an accident. The faulty wiring on the boiler. There wasn't the slightest suggestion of—of anything else, was there?

Phoebe (*heavily*) No! (*With "brightness"*) No! There wasn't, was there?

Philip (*firmly*) No!

Phoebe No. (*With asperity*) Then why can't we accept the verdict and live happily ever after?

Philip Ask Pat.

Pat (*desperately*) I—I don't want to cause any trouble. (*After a slight pause*) I—I know the verdict at the inquest was—Accidental Death, but —I can't believe that it was.

Philip Can you believe—it *wasn't*?

Pat is silent

Phoebe You know damn' well we're *all sure* it wasn't.
Philip (*feigning surprise*) I wasn't aware . . .
Phoebe Boloney! Of course you were. (*Slight pause*) Can *you* honestly say you believe it was an—accident?

Philip is silent

No, of course you can't; nor can any of us.
Philip So—the assumption is that—we have a murderer in the Company. Do you think that's—*possible*?
Phoebe (*muttering*) It takes all sorts to make a world.
Philip And has Pat any idea as to which one of us it is?
Pat (*brokenly*) I—I . . .
Philip And are you going to tell us, or . . .

Philip suddenly breaks off, moves up, and looks off R and L

Phoebe (*surprised*) What . . . ?

Philip motions her to silence. After listening for a moment longer, he suddenly moves quickly and silently off L

From off L there comes a quick, short gasp of alarm, followed by a short scuffle, during which Philip's voice is heard in broken sentences

Philip (*off L*) What are you . . . ? You know very well I . . . Now don't be stupid. You'd better come and explain.

Phoebe and Pat have risen, and from where they are standing, are looking L

Phoebe What on earth . . . ?

Philip returns, bringing Alan with him, held firmly by one arm. Alan is looking somewhat scared

Pat (*seeing him, brokenly*) Alan!
Alan (*to Philip, truculently*) All right! Let go of me. I shan't run away. Why should I?
Phoebe What *is* all this?
Philip (*releasing Alan, but staying by him*) Our young juvenile was out there—(*jerking his head L*)—listening. (*To Alan*) Weren't you?

Alan is silent

And when he saw me, he tried to make a bolt for it. (*Again to Alan*) Why?
Alan I—I wasn't—really listening.
Philip No? Then it's the best bit of acting I've ever seen you do. (*Slight pause*) You know damn' well you were listening. Admit it.
Alan (*truculently*) All right then. I was—in a way.
Philip What are you talking about—"in a way"? There's only one way of listening that I know of, and you were doing it perfectly.

Alan (*hesitantly*) I mean—I hadn't come to the side of the stage *deliberately* to listen.

Philip (*sceptically*) No?

Alan I—I was on my way out—and I happened to hear Pat say . . .

Philip (*breaking in*) On your way out? I thought I said you were not to leave the hall?

Alan (*testily*) I was only going to the shop at the corner to—(*he hesitates, then mumbles embarrassedly*)—to get some sweets.

Philip (*almost a howl*) For—God's—sake!! To get some sweets!!

Alan I—I . . .

Phoebe (*placidly*) What kind? Mints with the hole in the middle?

Philip (*roaring*) Phoebe!

Phoebe I *love* those!

Philip moves up, then down—speechless

Philip (*at last, coming to Phoebe's side; almost in tears*) Phoebe—will you please—*please* stop giving us your "Miss Marple" performance.

Phoebe (*crisply*) Certainly—when *you* stop giving us your "Inspector Barlow"!

Philip moves up and down again—again speechless

Alan (*at last, to Philip*) Do you—do you want me to go?

Philip (*not quite recovered*) What?

Alan Shall I go up to the dressing-room again?

Philip I think it would be a *very good* idea.

Phoebe (*quietly*) Do you? I don't.

Philip (*whimpering*) Oh, God!

Phoebe In fact I'll stick my neck out farther and say it's high time you got everybody here.

Phillip Everybody?

Pat (*under her breath*) Oh—no!

Phoebe (*practically*) Oh, *yes*! Everybody—including the theatre cat if there is one—and let's bring this matter out into the open—(*slight pause*) —whatever the consequences.

Philip And suppose we find somebody did—you know?

Phoebe *I* know. And I know what the result would be. As a "Society for the Purveyance of Dramatic Art"—we'd be finished.

Pat (*desperately*) Look! Why not let me just—resign from the Society? (*Quickly*) I couldn't carry on—believing what I do, but—with me out of the way . . .

Phoebe Everything would be hunky-dory—is that what you think? Do you seriously imagine we could carry on as if nothing had happened, knowing that we were all suspecting each other of—of murder? You're talking rubbish, child. (*Slight pause*) No. Which ever way you look at it, things don't seem too healthy for our little fellowship of players.

There is a pause

Philip (*at last, quietly*) Alan!

Alan Yes?

Philip (*quietly*) Go and ask the others to come here, will you?

Alan begins to move up R

Don't say anything about . . . (*Almost inaudibly*) Just ask them to . . . (*His voice tails away*)

Alan exits R

There is a definite silence. Philip moves restlessly

(*At last, quietly and sincerely*) You and I more or less started this Society, didn't we, Phoebe—ten years ago.

Phoebe (*also quietly*) We did.

Philip We've had our ups and downs. Sometimes I've wondered if it was all—worth while, but—I'd miss it now. After all I've no other—hobbies —pastimes.

Phoebe I suppose you could—as a last resort—take up bowls. That is, of course, if you're still around!

Philip Still . . . ? (*Muttering*) Oh, I see what you mean. (*Explosively*) But, good God! Surely nobody's going to suggest that *I*—Smith—that *I* . . .

Phoebe I'm not saying you'll be the firm favourite, but you'll be backed for a place.

Philip But that's . . .

There is the sound of footsteps pattering down a staircase off R, *and Doris's voice*

Doris (*off; loudly*) Thank you, Alan! Don't say they've got to my entrance at last! (*Louder*) Coming! *I'm coming!*

Doris sweeps on from up R, *reading from her script and acting heavily*

(*As she enters*) "Henrietta, you utter bitch! (*She moves to near the chair by the table* LC) What have you been telling that damned Inspector about me?" (*Shen then realizes the chair is not occupied. She looks round the stage, then in her natural voice, blankly*) Where is she?

Philip (*raising his voice a little*) What do you imagine *you're* doing?

Doris I'm making my entrance in this act! I'm supposed to come down to right of Henrietta—*Margaret*—but she isn't here!

Philip (*barking*) We are *not* rehearsing!

Doris Not? But Alan met me on the stairs just now and said I was wanted on stage, so naturally I thought . . .

Philip (*almost piteously*) Please—please . . . Forget it! Forget it! Just—sit down and forget it!

Doris But . . .

Philip (*bawling*) Sit down!

Doris collapses into the chair

Philip (*after moving to Phoebe, wearily*) Come to think of it, a life sentence would be a piece of cake compared with *this* caper, wouldn't it?

Phoebe Well, you've only got to stand up in front of us all and say, "God help me, I did it!" and no one will argue.

Margaret and Alan enter up R

Philip (*seeing them*) Ah, here you are! (*Looking round*) Where's Ronnie?
Alan (*almost nervously*) He's—he's gone over to the pub for a drink.
Philip (*angrily*) What? But I told him . . .
Alan (*overlapping*) He said he needed a quick one. Shall I go and fetch him!
Philip (*growling*) No! Leave him where he is. I couldn't stand his brand of comedy just at the moment. (*Speaking generally*) Sit down, everybody, please.

All sit, except Philip. After a slight pause, he moves C *and stands with his back to the footlights*

Right! Now—I've asked you all to come down here to tell you—(*with a look towards Alan*)—if you haven't been told already——
Alan (*muttering resentfully*) I haven't said a word.
Philip (*continuing*) —to tell you that—Pat—(*he gestures towards her*) has decided she doesn't want to go on with this play. Furthermore, she wants to resign from the Players.

Eyes are turned on Pat, but nothing is said

(*After a slight pause*) She has her reasons, of course. (*To Pat*) Perhaps you'd like to . . . ?
Pat (*desperately, hedging*) I—I couldn't do this play—not now. All the dialogue there is about—about death—not after what happened to . . .
Phoebe (*impatiently*) For heaven's sake, girl, why don't you come out with the truth? Tell them why you're really resigning.

Pat is silent

Phoebe (*to Philip*) You tell them.
Philip (*after a slight pause*) Despite the Coroner's verdict, Pat doesn't believe that Smith's death a fortnight ago *was* an accident. (*Slight pause*) She believes he was murdered.

No reaction from anyone

And that one of *us*—murdered him.

Again no big reaction

(*After heaving a big sigh*) And it's obvious from your reaction—or lack of it—that you all think the same.

Silence

Doris (*at last, to Philip*) What about you?
Philip *What* about me?

Doris I know you couldn't have done it, neither could I, but do *you* think
that somebody—one of the others—did?

Phoebe (*fairly sharply*) Why do you say that? That Philip couldn't have
done it? Or you for that matter?

Doris (*calmly*) Because, darling, Philip and I were *here*—on the stage—
when Smith came up those steps—(*pointing*)—and went down to the
kitchen. We were *still* here—a couple of minutes later—when Pat
came and told us that he was dead. So—you see?

Phoebe (*calmly*) I may be very dense, but I *don't* see.

Doris (*almost angrily*) Oh, for God's sake, Phoebe . . . !

Phoebe Smith wasn't stabbed in the back, you know; or shot through the
heart.

Doris Meaning . . . ?

Phoebe Meaning—he was electrocuted. Ergo—if he was murdered, whoever was responsible didn't have to be there in the kitchen at the time of
Smith's—exit from this world. In fact he'd take good care to see he
wasn't. Having set his trap, he'd make sure he was as far away as possible when it went off. (*To Philip*) So, Philip, darling, if you were thinking
of getting your halo out and polishing it up, I'd forget it, if I were you.

Philip (*after a slight pause*) We *all* had the *opportunity*—but as to—motive
—well . . . (*He pauses*)

Doris (*to Phoebe*) What about me, Phoebe? Do you think I might have
done Smith in?

Phoebe Yes. *If* you had a reason.

Doris But I hadn't.

Phoebe Then, obviously—you didn't.

Philip (*in exasperation*) But that's just it! That's what I *cannot* see! What
reason could *any* of us have to murder the man? It doesn't make sense!
I *know* he—he drove me mad every time he spoke to me, and I was
beginning to hate his guts, but—dammit!—you don't murder someone
just because you can't get on with them—at any rate, not within the
first couple of hours of meeting them you don't. (*Emphatically*) *And
that's the whole point!* We may *all* have disliked the fellow, but—he was
a *stranger* to us. We'd, none of us, ever even seen him in our lives before.

*There are murmurs of agreement from all except Pat and Phoebe. Phoebe is
sitting with her head lowered. During the murmurs, Pat looks towards Phoebe
for a split second. There is a slight pause*

Pat (*quietly, nervously*) Philip . . . !

Philip (*turning to her*) Yes?

Pat That—that isn't true.

Philip What isn't?

Pat That none of us had ever seen Smith before.

Philip *What?*

Everybody reacts except Phoebe, who is still sitting with her head lowered

Pat (*after a slight pause, turning to Phoebe*) Phoebe—I'm sorry, but . . .

Phoebe raises her head slowly

Philip (*to Pat*) Are you saying that Phoebe . . . ?

Pat (*after moving to Phoebe's side, quietly*) It's been torturing me, Phoebe, ever since Smith—died; knowing that you . . . (*She almost breaks down*)

Phoebe takes one of Pat's hands in hers and squeezes it

I came through the front of the hall to rehearsal that night, remember? You and Smith were up here on the stage—just the two of you. I—I couldn't help overhearing what you said to him.

Slight pause

Philip (*quietly*) What—did she say?

Pat (*after looking at Phoebe expectantly*) Phoebe—don't make *me* tell them, please, darling. (*She moves away*)

Phoebe (*at last, with hatred in her voice*) I said that if ever I got the chance to do him an injury—I'd do it!

Exclamations from all but Pat

Philip So you—did know him?

Phoebe *Know* him!! (*Slight pause*) He was responsible for—my son's death.

This is a bombshell to everyone

Margaret (*moving to Phoebe and putting an arm round her*) Phoebe . . .

Doris But, Phoebe—we didn't know you ever had a son—or that you'd been married.

Phoebe I—(*she runs a hand across her brow*)—Barry—that was his name, Barry—he was—illegitimate.

Everyone reacts

That's why I never spoke about him to anyone—not since I came to live here—after his death.

Philip (*after a slight pause, gently*) But—Smith—how does he . . . ?

Phoebe (*cutting in*) When Barry was born—that was when I gave up the stage—I had to—it was too precarious. I had to get a job with a regular salary. I got one in an office—in Chester. Barry and I lived there for fifteen years. (*Slight pause*) Barry went to a good school—he was an intelligent lad—inclined to be a bit—nervy—sensitive, but he was happy enough. Enjoyed his school life until . . . (*Slight pause*) During—what was to be Barry's last year there—Smith got the job of school janitor. Somehow, Barry fell foul of him very soon after he arrived—he annoyed him in some way or other—something very trivial—but Smith got his knife into him—and did everything he could to make the lad's life a misery. Then—God knows how—he found out that Barry was—illegitimate—and from then on he made the boy's life a hell. It wasn't long before all the school knew about him—he acquired a nickname—"The Bastard"—and—(*slight pause*)—schoolboys can be devilish cruel without really realizing it—lads who had been his friends, were soon—egged on by Smith—were soon being as swinish towards him as Smith himself. (*Slight pause*) I never knew a thing about all this until . . . the night before he died. I suppose he'd just reached the end of his tether, because he broke down completely that night and told me all about it. And that —because of it all he'd—somehow got on to drugs. You can imagine how I felt—but I tried not to let him see—I told him not to worry; that I would go and see his headmaster the next morning. He *begged* me not to do that; said it would only make matters worse for him if I did, but —I wouldn't listen to him. (*She pauses, then continues quietly*) The next morning, when I went to his bedroom to call him—he wasn't there. (*Slight pause*) He was found that afternoon—in the river—drowned.

Margaret (*under her breath*) Suicide! Oh, no!

Phoebe (*hysteria creeping into her voice*) Suicide? It was murder! Smith murdered my son just as surely as if he'd stuck a knife in his back! (*With exasperation, and brokenly*) Oh, God, and that's a line from some damn' play or other! (*She sobs very quietly into a handkerchief for a moment or two, then pulls herself together, and, after dabbing her eyes, puts the handkerchief away and looks round at the others. Very genuinely*) I'm sorry for the—histrionics. I didn't want to tell you, but . . .

Pat (*wretchedly*) It was my fault. I forced you to. I'll never forgive myself. (*She is almost in tears*)

Phoebe (*with mock severity*) For heaven's sake, child, don't *you* start!

Philip But, Phoebe—I'm sorry to ask you this, but—are you telling us that —because of what happened—you killed Smith?

Phoebe No—I regret to say—I didn't. (*Slight pause*) I can't prove that, of course. I can only tell you that if I'd had the opportunity I wouldn't have hesitated for a moment. (*Slight pause*) But I *couldn't* have done it —not the way it *was* done. I know nothing whatsoever about electricity —can't even mend a fuse. If I'd tried to mess about with that boiler, I'd most likely have ended up by killing myself.

Philip So we're back to square one.

Phoebe If you believe me—yes.

Philip Of course we believe you—I do, anyway.

Phoebe (*quietly*) Thank you.

Philip I—(*hesitating*)—I suppose no—one's prepared to—admit they killed Smith? (*Grinning*) Don't all answer at once!

Doris I've got a suggestion to make.

Philip What's that?

Doris Let's forget all about Smith and get on rehearsing this damned play. (*She holds up her book*) After what Phoebe's told us, do any of us care if Smith was murdered—or by who—er—*whom*? And I don't see how we're ever going to *find out whom*—er—who—whom . . . (*Giving up the grammatical struggle*) Oh, what the hell! (*Holding up her book again*) Now—in this masterpiece—it's a piece of cake! In Act Three, the Detective Inspector discovers that *Henrietta* was being *blackmailed* by the murdered man. He traps her into confessing and, before you can say, "Bob's your uncle", she's taking a flying leap over the extremely convenient balcony Right Centre, on to the concrete terrace below, *and voilà!* Quick Curtain! End of play! All go home!

Philip (*suddenly*) Good God!

Doris What is it?

Philip (*after a slight pause, quietly*) Blackmail!

Doris (*prattling*) That's right; in Act Three. The Inspector discovers . . .

Philip waves her to silence, then stands quite still for a moment, in thought. He then looks towards Margaret

Philip (*after a long look at her, quietly*) Margaret . . . ?

Margaret Yes?

Philip moves to Margaret before speaking

Philip The night Smith was killed—*you* said something to *me* about—blackmail.

Margaret (*quietly*) Did I?

Philip Yes. (*Slight pause*) It was after you'd shown me my scarf. You'd told me Doris had snatched it from whoever had attacked her. Remember?

Margaret Yes.

Philip And you went on to say that Smith knew it was my scarf, and that he knew it was I who had attacked Doris. And *I* said—if he was thinking of going to the police with that tale, I was going to break every bone in his body—or words to that effect.

Margaret Well?

Philip It was then you said, "There's not the slightest likelihood of his going to the police. *Blackmail's more in his line.*"

Margaret Did I say that?

Philip You did. *Why?*

Margaret I can't think *why*.

Philip (*sardonically*) Try.

Margaret (*flaring up a little*) What's all this about? Why the third degree? Are you making out that . . . ?

Philip (*topping her in a raised, but controlled voice*) All I am doing is asking you to tell me why you said what you did. You must have had a reason, and the only one that occurs to me is, that you *knew* he was a blackmailer. Well, *how* did you know? You can't tell by looks. You can't see a stranger walking down a street and point to him and say with certainty, "That man is a blackmailer!"

Margaret (*suddenly shouting, as she rises and moves away*) Oh, for God's sake—*shut up!* (*Almost with venom*) Don't you *ever* get tired of the sound of your own voice?

Philip (*stung, shouting*) Margaret!!

Doris (*under her breath*) Blind O'Reilly!

Margaret (*still with raised voice*) Why can't you do as Doris suggests—stop all this damned nonsense and get on with the rehearsal? That's what we're here for, isn't it—to *rehearse*! *Not* to watch you giving a fifth-rate performance of prosecuting counsel.

Philip (*grabbing her arm*) You're going to answer my question! How did you know . . . ?

Margaret (*tearing herself free of his grasp*) Leave me alone!

Philip I've got to know! I've got to know!

Alan suddenly rushes forward, grabs Philip and spins him round

Alan (*shouting*) Leave her alone, d'you hear?
Margaret (*shouting*) Alan! Keep out of this!
Alan I'm not going to let this swine . . .

The next fourteen lines are taken at great speed, excitedly and almost overlapping

Philip (*cutting in; utterly bewildered*) What the hell . . . ?
Margaret Alan—for God's sake . . . !
Philip (*brushing Alan off*) Have you gone out of your mind?
Alan (*cutting in*) If you want to know—Smith *was* a blackmailer.
Margaret Alan, shut up!
Alan (*overlapping*) And it was Margaret he was trying to blackmail; Margaret and me!
Philip (*incredulously*) Margaret and—you? What the devil are you babbling about?
Margaret (*to Alan*) You damned young fool! Will you keep quiet?
Alan (*unheeding*) I love Margaret. I love her I tell you!
Philip *What?*
Alan And she loves me, don't you, Margaret?
Margaret Don't listen to him, Philip. He's talking utter nonsense!
Alan (*stung*) Margaret!!

There is a sudden silence, and a pause. Philip turns slowly and looks at Margaret, almost in disgust

Philip (*at last, slowly and quietly*) You and—and this—kid! Oh, my . . . God!
Margaret You've got to listen to *me*. There was nothing—it was just a—a stupid—flirtation—nothing more.

Philip lowers his head

(*Desperately*) I—I suppose I was to blame. I shouldn't have encouraged him, but . . .
Philip (*cutting in; sardonically*) Don't—bother to explain! (*Quietly*) I *do* know the plot of *Tea and Sympathy*—and *Young Woodley*. (*After a slight pause*) Smith—how does he fit into—this romance?
Margaret (*desperately*) Philip, please—don't . . .
Philip You'd never met him—before he came here, had you?
Alan (*scornfully*) Of course we hadn't!
Philip (*turning on him, shouting*) I'm asking my wife!
Margaret (*hastily*) No—no—we—I hadn't ever seen him before.
Philip Then how could he possibly be blackmailing you? And what about?
Margaret (*almost wildly*) It's all so—ridiculous really; almost laughable.
Philip I'll be the judge of that—when I've heard the "laugh-line".
Margaret (*after controlling an outburst; quietly*) Before the rehearsal—that

night—before you or anyone else had arrived, Smith saw—he saw . . .
(*She cannot go on*)

Philip *What* did he see?

Alan (*half defiantly, half embarrassed*) He saw me with my arms round
Margaret.

Margaret (*to Alan, between her teeth*) *Will* you . . .

Philip (*cutting in; mockingly, to Alan*) He saw you with your arms round
Margaret. (*With a short laugh*) Was that *all*? (*Slight pause*) You weren't
—making so bold—as to kiss her?

Margaret (*angrily*) No, he was *not*! *Nor* were we rolling about on the floor
stark naked!

Alan (*shocked*) Margaret!

Philip (*to Margaret, in mock horror*) Please! Please! *Not* in front of—
(*with a gesture towards Alan*)—the child!

Margaret (*fuming*) I'm not going to stay here and . . . (*She begins to go*)

Philip You will stay! You *and*—Young Lochinvar!

Margaret moves down again

(*After a slight pause; more quietly and calmly*) I'm quite prepared to
believe that—as far as *you* were concerned—there was nothing but—
what you yourself called—a stupid flirtation. (*Turning to Alan and speaking quite sincerely*) And—let me say I'm damned—*damned* sorry for you.
I realize it might have meant more to you than that, though God knows
what you thought would come of it. But—(*gently*)—you'll get over it.
You will—you *will*—(*remembering*)—that is—so long as . . . (*He breaks
off and looks at Alan intently, then at Margaret. At last; quietly*) This—
blackmailing by Smith; we'd better hear more about it, hadn't we?
After all, we *are* probing into what we believe to be a murder.

Margaret (*horrified*) Philip, you can't believe that I . . .

Philip (*cutting in; quietly*) Blackmail—it isn't exactly Miss Christie's
prerogative for getting rid of someone, is it? It *does* happen in real life.
(*Slight pause*) To what extent was Smith blackmailing you?

Margaret He—he'd only just begun, but he would have gone on—
especially when he realized—as he soon did—that—my husband was
actually a member of the Society. But, all he'd had from me, so far,
was—it sounds ridiculous—a packet of cigarettes.

Alan He damned well forced Margaret to give him them.

Philip (*to Margaret*) And you were pretty certain he wasn't going to stop
at that—cigarettes?

Margaret Very certain.

Philip Well—there's *a* motive all right, isn't there?

Margaret (*raising her voice*) You can't possibly believe that *I* . . .

Philip It could have been a conspiracy between you both.

Alan (*with alarm*) What are you getting at?

Philip I'm trying to see it as the police would see it. You were—in love
with Margaret—you've admitted that. She was obviously going to be
blackmailed by Smith. Isn't it natural that you should do your damnedest
to prevent that? And, in what better way than the one that was used?

And, of course! Who better to do it than you—*than you*—a trained electrician!

Alan (*shouting*) You're accusing me! (*To the others*) God! He's accusing me!

Philip (*also shouting*) I'm not accusing anybody! But if the police are going to be dragged into this, isn't it best we *realize now* exactly what they *could* find out about *each one of us*?

Alan (*unheeding, shouting*) You'd like to see me in the dock, wouldn't you?

Philip (*loudly*) With my wife at your side as an accessory? Don't talk such damned rot!

Margaret (*fairly loudly*) Philip, you're being absolutely ridiculous. You know . . .

Philip (*ignoring her, cutting in, to Alan*) Did you go into the kitchen *after Smith had gone across to the pub*?

Alan Why? What . . . ?

Philip (*significantly*) *Bare wires!* That's what! And you're an electrician!

Alan What are you talking about? There weren't any bare wires!

Philip (*exasperated*) For God's sake! It was definitely stated at the inquest that the power lead was bare.

Alan Well, if I'd been there I'd've told 'em it damn' well wasn't—not when I saw it—nor when I left it. It was hanging loose, yes; and it was in a poor condition. The insulation was brittle—I could see that—but *it wasn't bare.*

Philip According to the inquest . . .

Alan And I'll tell you something else . . .

Philip (*impatiently*) One thing at a time for God's sake. You say the wire wasn't bare, but according to the inquest . . .

Alan (*almost yelling*) I don't care if it was according to St Matthew! *I know what I saw!* And if I'd been at the ruddy inquest I'd've told 'em!

Philip (*quietly*) And would they have believed you?

Alan (*shouting to the others*) You see? You *see*? He is trying to frame me! (*Turning on Philip*) All right! Go on! Get the police here. Go on! Get 'em! We'll see whether they'll believe me! *Go on . . . !*

Philip (*shouting*) Damn you, shut up, you young idiot! (*He grabs Alan firmly by the arms*) If you don't . . . (*More quietly*) If you don't stop this yelling, I'll . . .

A door is heard to slam at the back of the hall. Immediately afterwards Ronnie enters from the back of the hall, singing. The words are slightly slurred as he is a little drunk

Ronnie (*singing*)
"All the birds of the air
 Fell a-sighin' and a-sobbin'
 When they heard of the death
 Of poor Cock Robin
 When they heard of the death
 Of poor Cock Robin."

All on stage are peering out front. There is quite a buzz of inquiry

Philip (*calling*) Who's that out there?
Ronnie (*calling*) Still at it, are you? Queshioning and queshioning and queshioning?
Phoebe (*with a little laugh*) Oh, it's only Ronnie!
Ronnie 'S'right! 'S'only Ronnie! (*Singing*) "When they heard of the death of poor Cock Robin."
Philip (*fairly loudly*) What the devil's the matter with him?
Ronnie I'm soaked—that's what's the matter, soaked—(*he gives a giggle*) —inside and out! It's raining outside; did you know that?

No-one answers

(*As he comes slowly and a little uncertainly down towards the steps to the stage*) No, course you didn't! 'Spect you've been too busy theor—(*he has difficulty with the word*)—the-or-i-zing about Cock Robin! You know it all, don't you? (*Giggling*) But you didn't know it was raining outside. (*He is now near the steps*) Well, that's something even Ronnie can tell you. (*Singing as he mounts the steps with caution*) "When they heard of the death of poor Cock Robin."
Doris Ronnie, you old devil! You're tight! Come and sit down!
Ronnie (*coming on the stage, waving Doris aside*) Not tight! Not sober— (*he giggles*)—but not tight! Coffee! That's what I want—pull me together. I've come apart! (*He sings "Cock Robin" to himself quietly*)
Phoebe (*rising*) Shall I . . . ? The boiler is working again, isn't it?
Margaret Yes, and it's turned on.
Phoebe Right! Then I'll . . .
Philip (*coming to Phoebe and speaking fairly quietly*) Let him make it himself; it'll get him out of the way. We don't want him here. He'll only make himself a damn' nuisance. Anyway, he isn't concerned in this. (*He turns to Ronnie and speaks in an almost cajoling voice*) Ronnie, old man, why don't *you* go and make some coffee for yourself? In fact, make it for all of us and we'll come down and join you in a few minutes. How about it?
Ronnie (*heartily*) Good idea! (*He moves, then stops*) But the kitchen—the boiler?
Philip It's mended. Nothing wrong with it now.
Ronnie No?
Philip No. (*With shoo-ing gesture, wheedling him*) Off you go! Off you go!
Ronnie (*as he goes slowly up* C, *imitating Philip*) "Off you go! Off you go!"

Everyone on stage watches Ronnie. As he gets well up C *he stops suddenly and stands for a moment, then turns, chuckling to himself. He looks towards Philip*

(*Still chuckling*) You're a cunning devil, aren't you?
Philip (*blankly*) What . . . ?
Ronnie (*good-humouredly*) You and your—"who-dunnits"! Got 'em on the brain! "Agatha Christie-itis"—that's your trouble.

Philip I don't know what you're . . .

Ronnie (*overlapping*) 'Course you do! All this—questioning and questioning—you're loving it! You're playing your favourite part—the great, great detective! The great Hercule Poirot! (*He giggles*) And like Mr Poirot, you've set your trap, haven't you?

Philip (*impatiently*) God knows what he's babbling about.

Ronnie (*speaking generally*) Don't you see, all of you? In a few minutes he's going to get you down to the kitchen—the scene of the crime—(*including them all in a gesture*)—all of you—his suspects, and then—will come the big denouncement! (*From now on he gives an exaggerated performance of "Poirot"*) Mes amis! I 'ave lured you 'ere under ze false pretence, because I—Hercule Poirot, 'ave used ze little grey cells and can now reveal which of you is responsible for ze demise of ze un'appy Smith! Mais oui! Eh bien!

Doris (*applauding and laughing*) Marvellous, Ronnie!

Ronnie Thank you! (*Again "Poirot"*) I—Hercule Poirot, can say most definite 'oo stole in 'ere—just before Smith returned to continue 'is work on ze boiler—and made bare ze wire of death, and zen *switched ze boiler on*, so. (*He makes a switching gesture*)

Alan (*with a yelp*) My God! That's *it*! (*To Philip, wildly*) That's what I wanted to tell you, but you wouldn't let me!

From now on the dialogue is taken at terrific speed

Philip Tell me what?

Alan The boiler! When I was looking at it, it was *switched off*!

Philip (*exasperated*) What of it?

Alan It was switched off. Smith would've done that *before* he started to work on it, wouldn't he? And is it likely he'd switch it *on* again when he came back to get on with the job? I didn't do it. But *somebody* did! And —(*turning to face Ronnie*)—since he seems to know all about it—it must have been *Mr Hercule—ruddy—Poirot, here*!

Everyone exclaims

Doris Alan, have you gone out of your tiny mind? (*She laughs loudly*) Ronnie—our—burbling—bumbling, bless-his-heart, Ronnie—commit a murder?

Alan (*to Ronnie, excitedly, ignoring Doris*) Did you do it?

Philip Don't be a bloody fool! Of course he didn't!

Alan (*moving to Ronnie; completely carried away*) Did you do it? *Did you fix that wire and kill Smith?*

Margaret (*shouting*) Alan! Pull yourself together! ⎱ *speaking*
Alan Did you do it? *Did you do it? DID YOU?* ⎰ *together*

There is something akin to pandemonium as everyone shouts at Alan

(*In a moment of silence; almost screaming in Ronnie's face*) DID YOU?

Ronnie (*topping Alan in a wild yell*) YES! DAMN AND BLAST YOU, YES!!!

There is a stunned silence. Alan backs away from Ronnie, an almost scared "young lad". Ronnie is standing now almost limp, his face expressionless. Pat begins to sob, not noisily, but it is obvious that she might become hysterical. Phoebe moves near Alan, her eyes on Ronnie

Phoebe (*her eyes still on Ronnie; quietly but urgently to Alan*) Look after Pat!
Alan (*bewildered*) But . . .
Phoebe (*quietly, but almost impatiently*) Do as you're told!

Alan moves to Pat, sits by her on the form, takes her hand, and eventually his arm goes round her shoulders. Pat's sobbing fades away and, with Alan's arm around her, watches the others until the CURTAIN *falls. (The above business is secondary to the action that is happening elsewhere.) The moment Alan leaves Phoebe's side she goes to Ronnie*

(*Quietly, kindly, but urgently*) Ronnie—Ronnie, dear—this, this—is it another of your . . . ? (*A little louder*) Ronnie, are you playing the fool with us?
Philip (*moving a step towards Ronnie*) God! If you are . . . !

Margaret restrains him. Ronnie slowly looks towards Philip, then towards Phoebe, and shakes his head

Margaret (*brokenly*) Oh—God!
Philip But—why, Ronnie?
Ronnie Smith—he knew it was—was me who—attacked Doris.

Everyone exclaims

Doris (*wildly*) Ronnie, you're making all this up!
Philip (*overlapping*) For God's sake! You're not telling us that you're this —Prowler?
Ronnie (*not listening*) The night you lost your scarf—Smith was standing at the back of the hall. He saw me pick it up from under your chair— after you'd all gone and I was clearing the stage. I put it in my pocket intending to give it to you at the next rehearsal. (*Slight pause*) That's why I was wearing it when—that night—to make sure I wouldn't forget. (*Slight pause*) And that's how Smith *knew* it was me who . . . He must have heard us talking about the scarf. (*Slight pause*) When I went across to the pub to get him to attend to the boiler, he—threatened me; said he'd go to the police unless—unless I—(*slight pause*)—I had to give him every penny I had in my pocket there and then, and of course, I knew *that* was only the beginning. I *had* to do something about him—*had* to, and—I did!
Doris (*brokenly*) Ronnie—you—the Prowler—I can't believe . . .
Ronnie (*suddenly losing control and almost shouting*) No, of course you can't! Not your burbling, bumbling bless-his-heart, Ronnie! You're like all the other blasted women! None of you have ever thought of me as anything but a red-nosed comic—someone to amuse you, and fun to have around! (*Wilder*) A sexless bloody comedian, that's all I've ever

been in your—or any other woman's eyes! "Marry Ronnie? Go to bed with Ronnie? Ha! ha! ha! That's a joke to bring the curtain down on if ever there was one!" (*Almost viciously*) Well, let me tell you something! I don't want to marry any woman—or go to bed with her—*not now*! All I want to do is *hurt* 'em—hurt and humiliate 'em—the whole damn' lot of 'em, just as they've hurt and humiliated me! (*Slight pause; then with venom*) And I found a way to do it. (*Laughing*) Yes, by God! I found a way all right! (*Shouting*) And I'd've gone on doing it if . . .

Phoebe (*suddenly and authoritatively*) Ronnie—shut up!

Ronnie (*turning on her*) I won't shut up! I won't!

Ronnie glares at Phoebe, who returns his glare steadily. It is almost a battle between them. Then, at last, Ronnie's eyes fall, his body sags as he covers his face with his hands and begins to sob

(*At last—through his sobbing*) Oh, God! Oh—God! (*His whole body shakes*)

Everyone is transfixed

(*At last, brokenly*) The police—for God's sake—get them! Why don't you?

Philip (*to Phoebe, almost helplessly*) I suppose we . . . ?

Phoebe (*cutting in; firmly*) No!

Philip But . . . ?

Phoebe No! *We* can't do it. It would haunt us for the rest of our lives. (*Slight pause*) Let him—(*looking compassionately towards Ronnie*)—let Ronnie find *his own way* out of this. (*To Ronnie, gently*) Ronnie—you'd better leave us—go.

Ronnie (*after a slight pause*) You mean—give *myself* up—or what . . . ?

Phoebe (*after quite a long pause; slowly, and in almost a whisper*) Good-bye —Ronnie.

Ronnie, after a long look at Phoebe, turns and looks towards the others

Ronnie (*at last, scarcely audibly*) Good-bye.

Ronnie moves to the steps, goes slowly down them and, without turning, makes his way towards the exit at the back of the hall

Everyone is motionless, watching him go. After Ronnie has passed through the door, and it has closed behind him—

the CURTAIN *falls*

FURNITURE AND PROPERTY LIST

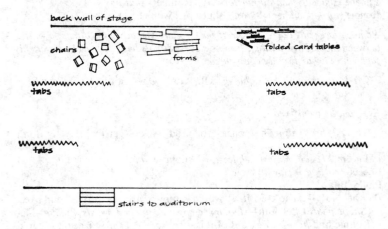

back wall of stage

chairs

forms

folded card tables

tabs

tabs

tabs

tabs

stairs to auditorium

ACT I

On stage: folded whist tables
small forms
bentwood chairs

Off stage: Scripts, books, writing pad (**Philip**)
Coil of electric wiring (**Smith**)
Biscuit tin (**Margaret**)
Packet of cigarettes (**Alan**)
Bottle of milk (**Phoebe**)
Shopping basket (**Phoebe**)
Briefcase with script, papers (**Ronnie**)
Script (**Alan**)
Red bloomers (**Smith**)

Personal: **Margaret:** wrist watch; handbag with script, cork-tipped cigarettes,
coins, lighter
Philip: cigarettes, matches, watch
Phoebe: handbag with script, umbrella
Pat: handbag with script

ACT II

Set: Bowl with bloodstained water, and first aid box on table
           Bandage on **Doris's** head
           Bottle of brandy and envelope in **Ronnie's** overcoat

Personal: **Doris:** square silk handkerchief
           Smith: cigarette behind ear

ACT III

Strike: **Philip's** table and chair
          Ronnie's table and chair
          Scripts, coats, etc.

Off stage: Script (**Doris**)

Personal: **Pat:** handkerchief

LIGHTING PLOT

Property fittings required: single unshaded bulb hanging from ceiling c
    Interior. An empty stage. The same scene throughout

ACT I   Night

To open: Single bulb on—no covering spots

Cue 1   **Margaret** and **Alan** embrace   (Page 2)
         House Lights come up

Cue 2   **Smith** exits   (Page 3)
         House Lights out, floats and battens up

ACT II   Night

To open: As close of previous act
No cues

ACT III Night

To open: As close of previous act
No cues

EFFECTS PLOT

ACT I

Cue 1   After CURTAIN up   (Page   1)
Door slams

Cue 2   **Smith:** "Yeh, I see!"   (Page   4)
Door opens, then slams

Cue 3   After **Smith** exits   (Page   8)
Door slams at back of hall

Cue 4   **Margaret:** ". . . ever let it start."   (Page   8)
Door opens

Cue 5   **Alan:** "You mean you . . . ?"   (Page   8)
Door slams

Cue 6   **Margaret** exits   (Page 11)
Door opens, then slams

Cue 7   **Pat:** "Isn't he . . ."   (Page 14)
Door opens and slams

Cue 8   **Philip:** ". . . the best of . . ."   (Page 21)
Prolonged noise of falling objects

Cue 9   **Philip:** ". . . devil are you . . . ?"   (Page 21)
Further noise of falling objects

Cue 10   **Smith** turns to exit   (Page 22)
Door slams

ACT II

Cue 11   **Phoebe:** ". . . that husband of yours?"   (Page 33)
Door slams

ACT III

Cue 12   **Philip:** ". . . stop this yelling, I'll . . ."   (Page 61)
Door slams

MADE AND PRINTED IN GREAT BRITAIN BY
LATIMER TREND & COMPANY LTD PLYMOUTH